TWICE FORGOTTEN

TWICE FORGOTTEN

John F. Kidd and
Erwin C. Winkel II, M.D.

To Jim best of luck
John Kidd, FNC, USN, Ret.

Jim
May you have a good read

VANTAGE PRESS
New York

FIRST EDITION

Published by Vantage Press, Inc.
419 Park Ave. South, New York, NY 10016

Manufactured in the United States of America
ISBN: 0-533-15193-7

Library of Congress Catalog Card No.: 2005902098

0 9 8 7 6 5 4 3 2 1

To Colonel Paul W. Tibbets, pilot of the Enola Gay, for his leadership of the crew that delivered the payload over Hiroshima. The atomic bomb saved the lives of at least 100,000 POWs scheduled for immediate execution upon the initial invasion of Japan. I was only one of those destined to be murdered. There were many lives impacted that day. This is the story of one. Sir, thank you for letting me see the flag of my country again, and live free.

Contents

TWICE FORGOTTEN

One
In the Navy

In the fall of 1939, on the occasion of Germany starting the war with Poland, over in Europe, I was one shaken teenager, jolted one night to think about the world harder than I ever had. Officially eighteen by military records, I was actually seventeen when I enlisted in the U.S. Navy for six years, sort of slipping in for adventure and to see the world. Tonight I was halfway through my basic training, glad to be here because, with an oversupply of men due to the Depression, they had made me wait a year. Sitting on the camp parade ground's curb watching the lights of San Diego backgrounding the ships in the bay, I said aloud, "Dang, maybe I've made a mistake."

Nobody around heard me, and I resumed my reasoning. The war's in Europe, a long way from here. Europeans have been fighting Europeans for centuries, and Asians have fought Asians for millennia. I won't give it a second thought.

Good it is that nobody can peer accurately into the future, for I would not have believed mine: the starvation, beatings, slavery, and experimental surgery I would receive as a prisoner of war from the enemy, or of being forgotten not once, but twice by our own government at critical moments. Unknown portents permit a pleasant present time.

As lights from the ships across San Diego Bay flickered on small wavelets, breeze-driven thoughts of personal purpose pushed away any fears I had for the future. In my life

I had overcome problems not common to the average kid my age—or so it seemed that night. Solving current problems gave me confidence with their resolution; but it never prevented new problems. The "aha!" of being part of a very big world had just hit me.

Enough of this philosophy. Right now I must get my tail up off the curb and traipse back to the barracks to complete my naval indoctrination. Weeks before, I had mastered basic training's first challenge: use of the Navy's traditional sleeping accommodation, the hammock.

No bunks graced the barracks, only hammocks stretched between points. I learned to crawl into this canvas tube. While grasping my hammock with one hand and the hammock next to it with the other, I had to swing my torso, buttocks, and legs upwards. If I was lucky, I landed inside my hammock. This Texas boy was glad the Navy had supplied a four-inch "belly band." Ordinarily, it was used in shipboard hammocks on rough seas. I tightened that band across my stomach so I would not accidentally roll over and fall six feet to the "deck" below, a marble floor.

Everyone mastered the art of swinging into his hammock in the first week. The art of staying there all night took longer. Some guys had rolled over in the night and were hung upside down by their belly band. They were rescued by their basic-training buddies, who we learned to call "shipmates." Once out of basic, I never got to use this hallowed sleeping tradition.

The number of shots given us while we walked a line with both arms extended amazed us. A Medical Corpsman would hit each arm at about the same time. I had seen needles many times in my stepfather's dental office, but a large, muscular six-footer in front of me passed out before the needle even got to him. We were directed to step over him until he came to. He got his shots while conked out.

My boot camp was the U.S. Naval Training Station, San Diego, California. The buildings still stand today down the road from the Marine Corps Training Center.

Our DI, drill instructor, was a naval chief petty officer, senior to all of us by a couple of decades. I had the fear of God placed in me by my parents: "Respect adults; liberally say, 'Sir' to them." I could not break the habit. The DI mistook Southern courtesy for my being a smart-ass. He made me pull extra guard duty several times.

Then came the fifth week of basic training, memorable not for the official tasks learned during the week, but for the liberty that weekend. Tradition says you must be "screwed, stewed, and tattooed" to be Navy. Those three initiations make you a real sailor in the eyes of other real sailors.

The first was accomplished in the traditional manner, and the second one, too. With drink enough for "stewed," I felt no pain with the third. So much "no pain" that I got two tattoos, American eagles. I could not know that these inked artworks on flesh would be an open invitation for extra beatings when you became a POW.

On my left forearm there was a flying eagle beneath a banner of stars, arrows clutched in one foot, and a U.S. Navy banner in the other. Below this proud bird were the initials DFK, as though I would forget who the patriot was.

On my right upper arm was a larger flying American eagle, with banner space to add my accomplishments later. Now I was really a traditional sailor.

DFK. Darwin Frost Kidd. This budding sailor made his very first "port of call" on February 10, 1922, in land-locked Tyler, Texas, to an established family, pioneers of the small town. My mother's home delivery was a planned event, the norm of the time before hospital deliveries, and netted me the name Darwin. Certain American events later nicknamed me "John," which I kept permanently. Inescapable Japanese events with a British correction would later give me the temporary name "Buttons." But on this day I began as Darwin Frost Kidd.

The signing of the Washington Treaty in its namesake city when I was but thirty-eight days old, had defused an intensifying naval arms race among the United States, Japan, and Great Britain in the Pacific Ocean, half a world away. Pacific peace seemed signed, sealed, and delivered.

From the time of my great-grandfather's return from the Civil War, there came children, and children of children—in our case, kids of Kidds. The Kidd family of Tyler branched into many businesses—a café, a hardware store, a cotton gin, and ten diverse dairy farms supplying milk to the creamery—hard working into their late sixties.

My mother's maiden name was Ruby B. Johnson. Her family was from Tyler, and two of her three brothers had served in World War I. She married my father, a classmate, in 1920 but divorced him in 1922, an act just not done. Any divorced woman was considered "shaded," out of tune with the rest of society.

A red-headed lady of Scotch-Irish descent, my mother did what she thought was right, tossing out the timely advice: "Stick with your man, no matter what." Legend is she caught the old man "hauling ice," so we suddenly left him for Houston and stayed with my uncle, her brother. "Hauling ice," 1920s slang for infidelity, was derived from the saying "When your husband's gone, the ice man is around." For home refrigeration, people used large blocks of ice placed in an insulated box, an "ice box." A man came around every day or so to bring fifty- or one-hundred-pound blocks of replacement ice. Sometimes the iceman replaced more than ice. My biological father remarried three times before settling down.

While we were living in Houston, my mother married my stepfather, on December 12, 1925, when I was three and a half years old. William M. Hill was a dental student, and the two knew each other in the everybody-knows-everybody ambience of Tyler. My stepfather's prominent family owned the lumber mill at the edge of town.

My biological father was willing for my mother to rear me, but his parents wanted me raised only in Tyler. My grandparents became possessive, so my mother went to court to get me away from them.

In the ensuing custody battle, I vividly remember one part. I, the five-year-old, was running around in the courtroom and hadn't seen my momma in a while. When she walked in and sat down, I saw her and I ran over. I hugged her and snuggled beside her. My paternal grandfather swears this was the reason they lost custody of me—even in a day when mothers usually won. The custody agreement had a stipulation that I would be allowed to visit my paternal grandparents each summer.

When school let out for the summer, I spent twelve weeks in Tyler with my grandparents, enjoying a warm and loving relationship. A cool relationship with my step-grandparents came not from animosity, but because I briefly saw them on my way to Dad's parents.

My land-locked origins came back to me in the next weeks as I continued to contemplate my part in our big world. Perhaps I was one of the little wavelets batted by the breeze I saw in the reflection of the ship's lights that night across San Diego Bay. Nothing more. That night I discovered me in the larger world. The Navy was a world of ships, our big brass favoring battleships as the wave of the future and judging aircraft carriers to be flimsy fantasy. Naval traditions die hard. In 1939, the larger the ship you were assigned to, the more important you were.

Naval traditions are hallowed, like a family looking out for its members. Best assignments were offered first to those with family ties to the ship, like a brother, cousin, or nephew. Before boot camp completion, they asked me if I had any relatives in the Navy. So I said I had a cousin, Gilmer Hester, on the USS *Nevada.*

"You want to be assigned to the USS *Nevada?*" they asked, offering me the rare opportunity to be part of a prestigious naval assignment, battleship duty.

"Yeah," I replied. I was the only sailor out of the whole boot camp that went aboard the *Nevada,* one of the Navy's finest battleships, because I told them Gilmer Hester was my cousin. He *might* have been a distant cousin, since we were from two families that had been in the same small town for generations. As far as I knew, we were probably not kin, but at least I knew someone aboard the mighty USS *Nevada.*

Two

Nevada Deck and Guns

I was part of the USS *Nevada* "deck force," a duty rousting you up each morning at five-thirty. By six, a bare-footed you, equipped with a scrub brush and sand, stood on the deck easing a wooden broom handle to a dent in the center of a six-inch-square sandstone chunk called a holystone. You go back and forth on a teakwood deck to clean it by sanding. A shipmate hosing the deck with salt water rinses the sand away while you stand there barefooted, your britches' legs rolled up. The low-fifties ambient air surrounding you is forgotten when cold seawater sloshes around on your feet. I figured I would freeze to death before breakfast. There must be a better way to make a living in the Navy.

One great distinguishing feature between sea duty on the *Nevada* anchored in Long Beach, California, and being in basic, was that of overnight liberty. You got to stay out for the whole night, doing ashore all those things that sailors traditionally do, and even catch a few winks in any time left over. As much as the fun of overnight liberty might have been, it was always duty first. You had to report to your duty station on time.

In scullery duty, I opened the lockers where all the flatware, pots, pans and dishes were stored. What I was doing was not only important, it was essential. Without me, the hot food would have been ladled into the crew's open hands.

Not a happy situation. Sailors on duty must eat on time, not necessarily fast, but on time because they relieve their counterparts to get their own meals. Regular shipmates could be hungry, only hungry, but those on duty would be hungry *and* late for duty or late for relieving their hungry counterpart. Tables stored in overhead swinging bins from the roof of the casemate for our six- or eight-inch guns were unfolded to provide three-by-eight-foot tables for a sitting crew. Mess cooks delivered food in tureens that were passed down for each to help himself. Breakfast, a first-class meal, consisted of powdered scrambled eggs, bacon, ham, and sausage, all spiced with ketchup, called "red lead."

One morning after an overnight liberty, I went to catch the first motor launch of the day. They leave hourly to transport crew to and from the ships anchored at bay, starting at 0600. I got to the dock a little early.

It did not leave on time. It left earlier. I saw the wake of the fifty-foot launch plowing through the calm bay as it headed for my ship. An hour later, the 0700 launch delivered me late to a thousand-plus angry shipmates.

A "lynch" party aboard ship awaited my return. Fortunately, someone else had unlocked the scullery department and issued the necessary equipment to feed the crew in my stead, but my absence had made everyone run late. The hungry crew probably thought about killing me, but they did something else. They gave me a nickname "John," as in "Johnny come lately." It stuck. I was never really crazy about my given name, Darwin, so I grew to like my nickname. After all, we called one another by our last names while aboard the ship, so I was still called "Kidd."

Ashore, while on liberty, I was "John." I cannot say how many times I had to listen to them laugh and tell how I got that name. It was a great icebreaker with the girls.

Space aboard the ship is limited, putting you closer to those around you than you want. It called for cooperation and understanding. Our earthly possessions, in a locker, twenty-four inches high, wide, and long, consisted of an original issue of one set of dress blues, one of dress whites, one each of "undress" blues and whites, and four pairs of "skivvies." We had dungarees for doing dirty work, like paint chipping, which we purchased on our own. The issued skivvy shirt looked like a white undershirt; the skivvy pants, like a pair of boxer shorts. If we wanted more clothing than issue, we could buy only whatever might be stored in our locker.

We washed our clothing in the personal laundry room but had the option of using the ship's laundry and paying for it. We personally laundered most of the time with soap bars strong enough to lather in salt water.

Shipboard sleeping is in close quarters, not in the basic training hammocks but near each other on a tier of three bunks, one six inches off the deck, one midway up, and the top one head high. Your ability to stay clean was paramount, because if you had any body odor, everybody around could smell you. The Navy even provided us with precious fresh water, not salt water, so we could shower every day. No ifs, ands, or buts about it, you had to be clean.

One guy in our division had a body problem of some kind, cause unknown. He would neglect to shower, and you could smell him two bunks away. A couple of the old hands gently warned him, "If you don't go down and scrub your stinkin' butt, we'll do it for you."

"Well," he replied, "that'll be the day! I'd love to live to see it happen."

So it did. His shipmates took him down and undressed him in the shower, with the water running. They scrubbed him with saltwater soap using a stiff bristle Kiyai brush that almost drew blood. After they finished, he never again missed his daily shower. Shipmate discipline was a necessity.

"Cousin" Gilmer picked up some body lice from going ashore somewhere and found them crawling in his groin area. Not wanting to go to sick bay and have this put on his medical record, he decided to treat himself.

Ships have rings around the portholes, and the expansions are all brass. The deck hands polish this with bright work polish, a solution of benzene and a bit of everything else to make the brass shine after you buff off the polish's temporary pink coating.

One night after everyone had sacked out, Gilmer decided to treat his crabs with bright work polish out of a pilfered can from his polishing duties that day. He stripped down, soaked his handkerchiefs with polish, and was rubbing it all over his body when the stuff started burning. We are three decks above the showers, which could only be reached by going down ladders in the hatches. He skipped into the hatchway and grabbed the rung at the opposite end of the opening, swinging down to the deck below

"Gangway. Gangway!" he screamed, swinging down below the decks buck naked. The Navy in those days was composed of men only, no coeds. He showered off the bright works. It relieved him of his "guests," but it almost got rid of Gilmer.

Amid the swabbing, team loading of the big guns, and shore leave, there was the quieter, personal side of naval life. The sea was our connection to the great big world out there just waiting to be seen. There was also a connection to something greater than the sea taking us to foreign shores. Faith in the Almighty. Faith was a personal thing. I preferred to express my belief privately, but I did attend the church services. They were usually held midships or on the quarterdeck, out in the open air. If it rained, the services were moved to the gun casemates, where we assembled to eat.

In none of my upbringing in Houston did I ever attend church or Sunday School with my mother or stepfather. They were neither antireligious nor had they anything unpleasant to say about organized religion. On Sunday mornings, we did other things.

On the other hand, when I went to my grandparents in Tyler, it was a different story. Each and every Sunday, come rain or shine, they attended St. Paul's Methodist Church, and sat in the same pew each time. Their faith was as sturdy as the Whippet car that they drove to church.

I dressed up special to go, but one Sunday my face wasn't washed clean enough for Grandma. She tongued her handkerchief and washed the smudge away. Ugggh! Never again did Grandma have to spit-bathe my face. I learned.

One Sunday in Houston, when I was nine years old, I dressed up in my knickers like I always did in Tyler with Grandma, made certain my face was clean, and walked alone a dozen or so blocks west of my home to the largest church in the Heights, Baptist Temple on 19th Avenue. I saw a baptism by immersion in a large tank behind the choir loft in the sanctuary. Whatever words went with the ceremony were undoubtedly the most important part, but the quantity and use of water impressed me. I didn't know how to swim.

I could not stop talking about what I saw. I was enthusiastic. I was shaken. I was scared of drowning. I told my mother about it in the greatest of detail.

"Boy," she said, "you ought to be a Methodist. They baptize by sprinkling."

With forty percent of the crew ashore on liberty, the attendance of those left was usually fifty to a hundred strong. We wore undress blues or undress whites, depending on the seasons. "Undress" is similar to "dress" uniform, but of lighter material, and without stripes on the sleeves or collars. Our sailor hats were off during the services, sitting in our laps or tucked in our trousers. Hats were always worn on the ship to properly salute an officer.

The chaplain served for all three government classifications of religious practice, Catholic, Jewish, and Protestant, the last meaning whatever else did not fit into the first two. Sea breezes and ocean sounds backgrounded the service of the day, and I thought of where I was rather than reminiscing of church at home with Grandma. The one thing common to all religions ashore was never done. No collection plate was passed. At the end of the service, we returned to "covered," hats back on for duty.

The major firepower of the USS *Nevada* consisted of ten sixteen-inch guns forward and aft, mounted on four turrets, three barrels lower and two upper. Control of all was in the hands of the pointer and trainer, who set the elevation and deflection of the gun barrel on orders of the central firing officer. The gunnery officer could fire them simultaneously.

Long before target acquisition and weapons discharge, there was the matter of loading the ammo from its storage in the magazine. My battle station was the "handling room," directly below the turret in the bowels of the ship, far below the water line and just above the bilge.

Ammo consisted of the projectile to hit the target and bags of gunpowder, called "charges," to energize. They would travel to the turret in separate conveyers with an isolated compartment for each bag to minimize destruction in case of an accidental discharge.

I handled the charges one at a time, very carefully, I might add. From the storage in the ship's magazine, I loaded the gray silk bags into the special conveyer for its trip up to the turret.

Each bag had a stripe of black gunpowder at one end that had to be placed towards the breech, or back of the gun. It ignited the white, or "smokeless," gunpowder when the electronic charge was applied.

In practice gunnery, the charges weighed sixty pounds each; in combat, the service charges weighed 110 pounds each. Six of the appropriate-sized bags were put through the open breech to energize the chosen projectile before them. A ramrod pushed bags and projectile together to the ignition area in the barrel. The ramrod assembly was then folded out of the way, and the breech was closed and locked. In combat, six 110-pound charges could fire a 2,500-pound projectile out of the sixteen-inch barrel twenty-five miles down range to the target, usually another ship. The projectile was either armor-piercing or contact-exploding, depending on need.

As time went on, I disliked being closed in that tiny room down below the water line. I decided to find some way to be moved out of my battle station in the first division.

In 1940, the Navy published a notice of getting a draft up to go to China. Volunteers. I thought that ought to be a lot of fun. China, here I come! I was glad they could use me somewhere other than in the handling room.

The idea of seeing a part of the world I had never seen before intrigued me, and doing it at the request of my country seemed downright patriotic. As far as I knew, Asia was a long way from the war raging in Europe.

The steps for transfer seemed simple enough. Get the permission of your immediate superior officer on a transfer slip, in my case Lt. Lou Hanson, the division officer in charge of gun turret number one.

He refused to sign my transfer request, the basis being that I was a trained crew member in the turret. We were due for gunnery practice this week, and he didn't want to lose my services. "Request denied."

Conventional naval wisdom was that the words "request denied" ended the matter. Perhaps I didn't know, or was stubborn, but I couldn't reconcile with the idea I should be denied something I wanted to do, especially by Lt. Hanson, who had earned from his crew a special nickname, "Stupid Lou." Even though he was a graduate of the highly respected Naval Academy, at Annapolis, he was the type of officer who made inane comments at times. Consider this. In drill practice during gunnery in the turret, he came up with the comment, "Awwright! We're gonna take a break, so rest on the double. We don't have much time." How can you rest on the double?

I thought that there was a higher being I could request this transfer from. At this point I was a seaman second, one grade above "whale dung" in the ocean. I took it upon myself to go into "officers' country" that Sunday morning.

Aboard ship the commissioned officers' territory was set aside from the crew. They had staterooms with two or three junior officers in each. The captain had a suite. Outside the captain's quarters, a marine guard stood duty twenty-four hours a day.

I went up into officer's country with my written request on the designated form, outlining what I wanted to do. I had no idea where or what was in "officers' country," but I found the captain's quarters with its armed Marine guard.

"What are *you* doing here?" the Marine crisply challenged.

"I've come up to see the captain," I replied.

"Well, who told you to come up here?"

"No one told me to come up here," I said. "I came up on my own."

Fortunately, the captain overheard our muffled conversation through the light curtain drawn across his hatch door.

"Sentry, what's going on out there?" called the captain.

"Sir, there's a man out here wanting to talk to you." The Marine looked mean. How dare this low-rank, low-life sailor invade the private moments of the captain? His eyes glared the message "Buddy, you are history."

"Send him in."

At this time I was only eighteen calendar years of age, nineteen on Navy paperwork. That was the highest ranking officer I'd ever seen. I was standing there, rigid as a board and scared half to death. I told him what I was doing there, that I had filed my request for transfer to the Orient, because I understood they needed men in the Orient.

"Well, present that to your division officer."

"Sir, I presented it to Lt. Hanson—"

"Well, what was his comment?"

"He told me, 'Forget it,' and marked it disapproved."

The captain said, "You got it with you?"

"Yessir," I said, and I showed him the request.

He took it and, while looking it over, said, "You really want to go to China?"

"Yessir."

"May I inquire why?" He studied the document. "On what grounds?"

I said, "Well, it's something *different*."

"That's grounds enough." He immediately marked my request "approved," and signed his name, "Captain Rockwell."

"Have a good day, son," he said. "And be careful."

I saluted him, turned around, and walked out. This was the turning point of my career. Years later, I ran into him, after he became an admiral. We both recalled this incident.

At the personnel office on the USS *Nevada*, I delivered my request to the yeoman on duty and said, "I'm going."

"Hell, yes. I guess you are," he said, hurriedly typing the order and all its necessary carbon-copy distributions.

I rushed back up to see Gilmer Hester, who was in the first division with me. My "cousin" was visibly shaken that I had been to see the captain. In disbelief he blurted out, "Boy, you got more guts than you got sense."

"Well, at least I got my transfer approved."

I rushed packing my sea bag and gear and made it ashore before the USS *Nevada* pulled anchor that evening for two weeks of gunnery practice.

I got a delay in route, as it is called in the Navy. I took my leave and headed to Texas, not to Houston, to see my mother or stepfather, but to Tyler, where I saw my dad and my grandparents. I phoned a girl I had known before enlisting in the Navy, who lived on a large farm with her parents. We went to a movie in a car borrowed from my dad. In ten days my orders called for me to go back to the West Coast and meet the USS *Henderson*, a transport ship.

Money was really tight. I was paid $36.00 per month. Newspapers carried ads where you could share a ride across the country with other people and split the cost. I joined a group going from Dallas to Los Angeles, so my dad, with new wife number three, drove me to Dallas. Of the whole trip, I remember only one of our conversations, but I remember it well.

"Son," he said, "I want you to clarify something for me about the Orient."

"Okay."

"Tell me if it is true that the Chinese women run east and west instead of north and south, willya?"

I was not sure of his directions, but his destination, if it was that, was achieved. I was thoroughly embarrassed in front of his new wife.

I joined the four other members of our party for the share-the-driving trip to Los Angeles, which cost around $17.00 apiece.

A bachelor cousin my mother's age lived with his sister in Los Angeles. He was a wheel with the water department, so I called him to spend one night with them. The next day I got a bus ticket to San Francisco.

I was eighteen, with very limited travel experience: Houston, Tyler, and Marshall, all in Texas. Boot camp in San Diego with a hitchhike afterward to Tyler. These places do not an experienced traveler make.

My orders said to "catch the USS *Henderson* in San Francisco." It gave a specific date and pier to meet the ship.

I get to San Francisco. I go to the dock. I stand there. Lapping twenty feet below the pier is San Francisco Bay, with plenty of cold waves, wind, and occasional fog. What it does not have is my ship.

Puny indeed was the question from Seaman Second Kidd, "If she isn't in San Francisco, where the hell is the USS *Henderson*?"

Three

A Naval Oriental Introduction

I am one panicked seaman second; clear orders, but no ship. I don't know what to do. Because of my limited world experience, I ran for the nearest family I could find and caught a bus back to Los Angeles.

My perplexed cousin delivered me to the recruiting station. The chief recruiter 's puzzled look melted into a smile. By hastily typing my transfer orders, the *Nevada*'s yeoman had entered the wrong dock number for the *Henderson,* due in from Bremington Shipyard in Washington State. "You could have learned this from the San Francisco recruiting office," he added.

I bussed back, but was three days late in reporting. I was immediately placed on report, which was almost as bad as a court martial.

"Sir," I said out on the quarter-deck, standing at attention before the Captain. "I was here, but the ship wasn't."

"You're supposed to find the ship. I find you guilty of reporting for duty late. You are restricted to the ship. No liberty while in port."

"Yessir." Not getting liberty made me no difference. All my money had been spent on bus fare.

"Turn around and look across the way, over to that island," he added. "That's Alcatraz, and if you do this often, you'll end up there. Dismissed!"

"Yes, Sir!"

After four more days in port, the *Henderson* got under way for Manila. While in the chow line on deck, I met a Marine from Texas as we steamed out of San Francisco Bay. As we passed down the line with our metal trays for lunch, one mess cook plopped on mashed potatoes, and the next server mashed an imprint in the heap for half a cup of greasy gravy. The next guy slammed on a pork chop, followed by the veggie server's contribution. Finally the last man topped it off with a piece of pie. Next, we found some place to sit down.

"Come on," I said to this buck private, "we'll go back and sit on the stern and eat off the bits." The stern is the rear of the ship. It has "bits," those standards on the deck for a line to moor the ship in docking.

The ship was pitching high and low a lot because, as you leave San Francisco, ocean currents flow together and bounce a ship like a pogo stick. Though I ate up a storm on this seesaw, he set his tray on the deck and ran to the other side to heave over the rail. He was seasick. We were sitting on the roughest part of the ship, the stern. To this day, I disclaim that I had any idea this would make him sick so that I could eat his pie, but it worked out that way.

In Honolulu we docked at a pier near the Aloha Tower and were met by hula dancers in grass skirts, tops, and leis. I did not see "battleship row" at that time, because the Pacific Fleet was still in Long Beach, California, nine months before coming to Pearl.

We were granted overnight liberty in Honolulu, an American-controlled territory, which contrasted to the nine P.M. curfews reserved for territory not so much under our control. My most lasting memory of Hawaii was of black sand filtering through my fingers on a beach somewhere. I thought all sand was tan, like in Galveston, Texas.

Transports had a top speed of ten knots, but the *Henderson* did less than her top for this routine six-week trip. My Marine buddy went on to Shanghai, and I debarked at Manila Bay into a naval motor launch that took me straightaway to the USS *Blackhawk,* AD9. This tender for thirteen destroyers immediately got under way for ports on the China coast.

On April 1, 1940, the USS *Blackhawk* had the Commodore's Flag on board, known as ComDesRon 29, Commander Destroyer Squadron Twenty-nine. For all the glory of first meeting the ship, damned if I didn't once again get put in the "first division," a euphemism for those who swab the deck. Okay. I scrub the deck again. No matter. Smaller deck. We're under way for China.

By custom, all quarter-decks were made of teakwood. Though steel plate was always underneath, teakwood shored naval tradition. Teakwood is best swabbed with sand and a holystone; metal decks, with a mop.

All the crew was older than I; I was the "kid" of the ship. Last names were used among shipmates while on board, so again I was called "Kidd." On shore leave, we called each other by our first names, and I preferred my nickname picked up on the *Nevada,* "John," to my birth name, Darwin. Though my drinking buddies called me "John," the girls tended to call me "Johnnie." Nicest of all, this crew didn't know the story of its origin.

In the past decade or two, some of the crew had established families in Manila. When our ship sailed for Chefoo, China, some of the wives went ahead by commercial ship so they could be together with their husbands on overnight liberty, since our Chefoo stay was for four months.

Along with the old crew was the old ship. The USS *Blackhawk* had a flank speed of nine knots, providing that the movie screen was also rigged as a sail. This banana boat, built in 1900, had been converted into a destroyer repair tender, a floating machine shop. She had no watertight integrity except for the powder magazine for ammo storage. When it showered, it rained to the keel.

Usually three of our destroyers would come in and tie up alongside of us whenever we were anchored as part of COMDESRON 29. Upon completion of repairs, they would depart for maneuvers with other divisions at sea.

If major repairs or dry docking were necessary, the destroyers went into the Cavite Naval Yard in Luzon, across the bay from Manila. These "four-stackers" of World War I vintage generated a published written order forbidding the use of air hammers when they went into dry dock. Their hulls were in such bad shape that a chipping hammer might knock a hole in them. These rusted hulls decried the seaworthiness of our vintage Asiatic Fleet.

In April 1940, we got under way for China. The further north we went, the more bizarre some of our crew became. It was unnerving to see guys perched on top of radiators wrapped in blankets. One yeoman sitting in the quarter deck office sneaked his fingers to typewriter keys from under a woolen blanket. Shivering, without fever, they were freezing to death. The temperature in the upper thirties was a definite change from the ninties of Manila. My seeing the effects of sudden climate change for the first time was unnerving. Our tropical crew had raced to northern latitudes too fast, six days of steaming to reach Hong Kong.

As one of the barefooted deck force holystoning the teakwood one morning, I noticed guys inside the flag office on the quarter-deck still asleep, oblivious to our cold deck wash-down. Office sailors complete their day of desk duty, clear off the tops, and replace papers with mattresses for the night. Their work area is also their sleeping quarters, for the desks are permanently attached to the bulkheads, ship parts that landlubbers call the "walls." Wet, cold, and awake on the outside, I looked in and thought, *Theirs is the type of duty I'm looking for.* I decided to strike for yeoman.

At first you are an apprentice without a rating. Your training in that field is called "striking," and once each three to six months exams are given. If you pass the exam, you become rated in that field. Since I could type and liked the organization of office work, it would be for me.

Our stop at Hong Kong en route to North China really mystified me. I was dumbfounded to see the Chinese come out to the ship in small sampans and stop at our garbage-disposal chute. After the meal served had been eaten, mess cooks scraped all the left-overs from the plates into a large garbage cans to dump overboard. These slop chutes for garbage disposal on the stern opened six feet above the sea. After sloshing down the leftovers, anything clinging to the chute was washed away with sea water from a four-inch fire hose. Always, two or three sampans with Chinese holding buckets beneath the chute caught the falling scraps of food before the hosing down. They took our garbage ashore and sold it as food to other hungry Chinese.

One wrinkled old lady we called "Slop Chute Mary," a toothless, thin, and weathered dweller who spoke no English, had been meeting our ship for years. She would wave to us and we tried to dump it toward her dish pan held high over her head as she balanced on the rocking deck of her sampan. Slop Chute Mary was sort of our pathetic port pet.

Ashore in Hong Kong for my first liberty in six weeks, I had finally planted my foot in China. In one of the many bars, I met a Sapper from the British outpost who took me over to the British enlisted men's club. They served us some small things that looked like skimpy Texas hotcakes, my first exposure to the English national food, crumpets. We talked a bit over tea, mostly about the war in Europe, how his family fared in the Nazi bombing of London. We walked around town, with no place to go and not much money. The exchange rate there was four to one—four Mex to one gold, i.e., four Hong Kong Dollars for one of ours. The U.S. dollar was referred to as "gold."

Street urchins would come up to you and say, "Hey Joe, you likie my sister," and try to sell you her services. That perplexed me so I questioned the hands aboard ship. They informed me that a female over there was considered zilch, often being sold into prostitution at about the time of puberty. They informed me you could buy a female teenager for $120.00. This was totally new to me. Nothing I learned in school or basic prepared me for this.

One of the sailors took a young Chinese boy up on his "Hey Joe" and followed him into a crowded alleyway, into a room of one of the hovels. In one corner sat a group of Chinese men around the table intently playing cards, probably relatives of the boy and his sister. In the other corner of the room was a four-poster bed with a young girl on it. A pull curtain suspended from the four posts surrounded the mattress for privacy.

Reluctantly at first, the sailor went over to the girl, and she drew the curtains together, separating her from the men playing cards, who seemed uninterrupted in both their conversation or interest in the game.

The sailor participated in sex with the girl, his rapid, high-interest, flaming fury of horny youth tempered a little with worry. The relatives outside the curtain were probably brothers or uncles. Back home, if someone were doing this to his sister or niece, they'd beat the crap out of him . . . "Ohh. Ahh. There. Done."

The young girl stepped out from the curtains afterwards, and returned with a bowl of water and a wash rag. After she had washed him off, he paid her price. He left the scene as he had come upon it, Chinese men in a card game at one side of the room, a young girl on a bed with an open draw curtain on the other side. It was as though nothing out of the ordinary had happened. He was but a ripple in their daily sea of life.

On this liberty I decided to permanently honor my place in life, the fleet of our nation, and the ship I had been assigned to. I added to the tattoo of the flying eagle on my right arm my personal message of where I came from. Above the eagle, I had them tattoo the words "U.S. Asiatic Fleet," and, below the eagle, "USS Blackhawk." I was a young salt, proud of my place in life.

Liberty until nine P.M. meant that you had to catch your naval motor launch for transportation back to ship then. Noon 'til nine meant that there wasn't enough time to drink as much booze as you thought you ought to have, because the only liquor you could bring aboard ship was what you had already consumed. For many sailors, what you drank made you a stumbling drunk.

Sometimes a half-dozen or so sailors passed out and lay on the deck of the liberty launch. The naval way of getting them back shipboard was to put a square cargo net on the deck and load about three or four sailors in the net so that none of their arms extended through the net. Then the four rings at the corners of the net were looped through by a hook on a cable. The shipboard boom lifted the cargo of sailors out over the motor launch.

As they dangled in a squirming pear shape over water, like so many fish caught in a net, the launch moved away. From the ship a four-inch fire hose shot cold seawater on the net and its cargo, until there was little certainty that they were now quite awake.

The boom gently swung them aboard ship and onto the deck, where they were awake enough to go below deck to get back to sleep. Rough as this wake-up call was, it probably saved many a sailor from passing out, vomiting while in a deep slumber, and choking on his own vomit. This, whether in the anesthetized sleep of surgery, or in the drugged slumber of too much alcohol can be such a lousy way to die.

Four

An Eagle on the *Blackhawk*

We departed from Hong Kong and went up to the northeastern coast of Asia, near the Russian border. Almost in the shadow of the Great Wall of China was Chingwantaw, and a rifle range used by the Navy. Recently I looked on a map of China and found no such city. I called the Chinese embassy in Houston, and a polite young voice told me, "Chingwantaw? Oh, sir, that was before my time."

I could see the Great Wall from where we were anchored, but since I was a year out of boot camp, I did not go ashore for target practice. The twenty live rounds I had fired during my training were considered "recent weapons experience" when compared to the "old salts" shipboard.

The Navy did not pay the guys before they went ashore to the range, so there was little money to spend, but you could purchase a girl's favors over there for a skivvy shirt. Nearly all guys returned shirtless from shore. With the phenomenal number of replacements, I am certain the paperwork in Washington bespoke of conspicuous skivvy shirt consumption in the China Sea theater. Washington may have concluded it was the Chinese weather, but it really was the Chinese "whether"—whether sailors had Chinese-girl fun.

Captain Harris was the skipper of the USS *Blackhawk*, but there was an executive officer on board named Commander Winn. He was a tyrant over his command and was considered weird and eccentric by most of the crew. Shipboard scuttlebutt was that he used to be a skipper. Supposedly he had severely damaged his ship in Honolulu during docking. Something like putting the ship *in* the pier instead of *at* the pier. He was found at fault, and the Navy sent him to the Asiatic Fleet as our executive officer for his punishment.

He had seven pots of live plants, zinnias or geraniums, growing near his shipboard office at the stern of the ship, which was also close to one of the "heads," where the sailors exercised their bathroom privileges.

This head could be entered from either port or starboard side and was a single narrow room running almost the width of the ship. One side had a shallow urinal, a slit trench for liquid waste. On the opposite side was a wide, U-shaped culvert-sized half-pipe to which standard toilet seats were attached. Clean sea water continuously sluiced through both watercourses and, when mixed with the waste, was pumped back into the ocean.

One day only six plants were astern, flapping in the breeze. A week later, five. Perhaps the executive officer's paranoia or his prior experience with common sailors prompted the presence of an armed guard for potted-plant protection. Sailors were given "extra duty" as a guard in that location. Some translated "extra duty" as "punishment duty," and the most common crime resulting from this duty was smoking in the head, strictly forbidden.

The only way to get off this "extra duty" was to catch someone else smoking in the head. Then your tour of "extra duty" ended, and his began. In this setup, the guard was more interested in watching for cigarette smoke from the head than protecting potted plants.

No doubt the plants were watched by more eyes than the executive officer and his guard. Nobody really knows what happened—perhaps the guard had to avail himself of the head. Whatever he did and wherever he was, when the guard walked away, *whoosh*! Over the side another plant would go. After three weeks, they all disappeared.

Somebody did it, but guilty shipmates secreted the details. That escapade came to mind years later when I saw the movie *Mister Roberts*. James Cagney played the eccentric captain of a naval support vessel. Our live *Blackhawk* experience with the Executive Officer's plants was mirrored in the movie scene where the captain's palm tree was tossed overboard.

We finished at the rifle range and sailed to Chefoo, China, summer-home port for COMDESERON 29, destroyers and tender. The *Blackhawk* had thirteen destroyers on rotation, with a maximum of four at one time tied to the tender. As we spent the summer of 1940 in the bay of Chefoo, the Chinese coast was captured and placed under the control of the Japanese Army. Every city we went into was occupied by a Japanese Army unit.

The Japanese Army and Navy were not necessarily coordinated. Unlike the army and navy of the United States, they were independent of each other. That explains how the Japanese Army would have the land control without their navy simultaneously controlling the sea at the land's end. We had not seen a single Japanese man-o-war in the seas of North China, but as we patrolled further south down the Chinese coast in mid-1940, we began to see some of Imperial Japan's warships.

On the other side of the world, European hostilities did not affect us. After invading Scandinavia in April of 1940, Nazi Germany's blitzkrieg of the low countries, Holland and Belgium, came in May. By June the British aid to France had ended in defeat. All of Britain's private civilian boats were called into action for the mass evacuation at Dunkirk. The eloquent Winston Churchill vowed, "We shall defend our island, no matter what the cost—we shall never surrender." President Franklin Roosevelt condemned all the war actions, but offered Britain our surplus materiel. All those events half a world away resulted in no orders to us indicating that we could be involved.

The politics of shipping in a world where some parties were involved in a war against others led to the concept of "free ports." In a free port, the war was forgotten. By mutual agreement, there was no fighting while in the port. Everyone restocked their ships stores, partook of liberty, and waited until they were again on the high seas before damaging each other. I did not fully understand the rules of the world when I was going through it. I guess the young never do.

When an American sailor went ashore in Japanese-controlled Chefoo, he traipsed through the outskirts of their bunkers and merely walked up the street. The Japanese had no checkpoint for Americans. The Chinese had no passport stations. The Japanese barracks were on one side of the dock area with sandbag-encircled machine-gun nests providing security. On the waterfront of Chefoo, we freely passed three such emplacements in one and a half blocks on our way to liberty in town. Being a seaman second, I do not know what protocol, if any, was used then to establish rapport between the U.S. Navy and the Japanese Army.

Chefoo had been controlled by the Japanese since 1939 with a full emplacement of their officer staff and enlisted personnel. Japanese control was better by day than night, because various Chinese rebel armies were still skirmishing with the Japanese. The Chinese Army was not a unified national organization, but a conglomeration of embattled warlords, some of whom were fighting among themselves when not battling the Japanese Army.

The Chinese would occasionally attack Chefoo and kill a few Japanese. None of the warlords were allied with the Americans, so their actions created no problems between us and the Japanese.

The strangest thing we experienced was the high level of entertainment that seemed to follow us from port to port. Welcoming us up and down the line at our destination ports was the same band of Russian musicians and ballerinas. The old salts pointed out that the Russian troupe, which had fled for their lives after the Communist Revolution, would traverse by land and sea to meet us.

Though the crew did not know where our next port was until we got there, the Russian band members always knew. They opened up cabarets in the local ballrooms. Fourteen-piece bands would play, and there were plenty of Russian ballerinas to "taxi dance" with. You paid one Mex for one dance. With the exchange rate at Chefoo being twenty of their dollars for one of ours, we were only paying a nickel per dance. The girls were white Russian refugees who had escaped from the Red Russians, those who favored communism.

Though liberty was granted from noon till nine, it was more like eight hours rather than nine that you were truly at liberty. The nine P.M. deadline meant that the Navy motor launch to return you to your ship left then. You had to be on the dock in plenty of time to board it. Thus you had to drink, dance, and do whatever in pretty much of a hurry. That may explain why so many of the sailors rapidly downed large amounts of booze with the expected result. Some got tight; others got downright potted. Those merely impaired helped their incapacitated buddies back to the ship.

One night as another motor launch was approaching and the usual line waited on the pier, there was a sudden outcry by a Japanese soldier behind us. Not knowing what was going on, I turned around very quickly. Standing up on the sandbag of a gun emplacement was a crocked Chief Petty Officer urinating on a Japanese soldier in the pit. The Japanese guard was yelling at him with anguish, disgust, and anger. Our sailors ran over and got the chief down off the sandbags and pulled him aside. Fortunately, the motor launch had arrived, and we jumped aboard and got out of there. We thought nothing more of it.

Sailors did their own laundry shipboard every third day. When the ship was in a Chinese port, that changed. Sailors sent their clothing ashore, where a full week's worth could be laundered, pressed, and delivered back to the ship for only twenty cents American. The efficient Chinese would even iron your undershirts, shorts, and skivvies. Commonly, half the clothing of a ship docked in any Chinese port was ashore at a local laundry. So it was for the *Blackhawk* crew at the time of the urination incident. The Japanese got quite pissed off about being pissed on.

Due to that incident, our laundry was frozen by the Japanese garrison in charge, and the Chinese were not allowed to deliver it back to the ship. We waited a couple days for our onshore week's worth of clothing, and then the captain or commodore called for a "landing party." It had to be with the commodore's approval because he was on board. Although the captain ran the ship, the commodore outranked him.

The landing party was armed with rifles and Thompson submachine guns. It marched as a unit, locked, and loaded in front of the block long Japanese garrison half a mile inland to the Chinese establishment and paid for our laundry. The party returned, eyeball to eyeball, past the armed Japanese, an inadvertent parade in review of two military units and three sets of uniforms, one pressed and neatly packaged. Our laundry returned shipboard without incident.

The venereal disease problem for sailors was controlled in Chefoo because the Navy ran a two-block square area of prostitution in houses of a gated community behind a wall. The Navy doctors examined all the prostitutes.

Anyone entering the restricted area, whether as participant or sightseer, surrendered his liberty card to the shore patrol on duty at the gate.

Afterwards, in order to obtain your liberty card, you had to utilize the services of the prophylactic station. This meant you injected your used or unused penis with Potagerol, a liquid medicine to disinfect any prostitute exposure you may have had. A rubber bulb on a 10cc syringe held a dark brown liquid with the viscosity of water. The point of the syringe was not a needle, but a thick, glass V-shaped end that was jammed to the end of your urethra. With the snug fit, a gentle squeeze on the rubber bulb sent the liquid through the urethral channel, the tube in the penis reserved for urination or ejaculation.

This was like urinating in "reverse gear" and was the most effective method of prophylaxis then in use, since condoms were not used. Intercourse *au naturel* was the order of the day, and this post-exposure treatment was used to prevent the serious consequences of syphilis and gonorrhea, the two most prevalent venereal diseases of the day.

The sailor's personal quest for pleasure was done in private, but his prophylaxis was completed under the watchful eye of the Medical Corpsman. Once the sailor came back out the gate, his liberty card was returned and his regular rights restored. Failure to follow this procedure resulted in arrest and court-martial.

We departed Chefoo and went down to the more modern city of Tsingtao, where wider-paved streets accommodated cars as well as rickshaws. Chinese dance halls, Russian cabarets, and various saloons provided us with plenty of entertainment.

We had been in Tsingtao three or four days when a bunch of our crew was on the beach, swimming and sunning along with a number of Orientals. The white sandy beaches greeted us like a tropical paradise, but there were no coconut palms. It was a warm summer day when we traded in our white dress uniforms for bathing trunks and splashed around with the natives. One of our sailors, who had consumed an ungodly amount of booze, put the make on this Oriental girl lying beside an Oriental man. Little did he know she was not Chinese, but Japanese.

The man resented the passes made to his wife, and got up and started screaming. The American sailor cold-cocked him. Other Orientals came up and helped their injured comrade to the hospital. No one could tell by the pair of swimming trunks this man had on who he was. Our sailors found out that not only was he Japanese, but he was also the commanding officer of the Japanese garrison in Tsingtao. The American sailors quickly gathered up their gear and left for the United States Army-Navy Club.

The sailors arrived at the Army-Navy Club and carried on as though our crew had been there all the time. A couple of shore patrol members were stationed outside the club, but they did not mark entry or exit times of patrons.

An hour and a half later, the Japanese military police marched up to the shore patrol area in front of the club. This Japanese officer with a sword at his side seemed to be in command. He walked up, said nothing, and began slapping our shore patrol. In that Japanese military officer's mind, he was closing the unfortunate beating incident at the beach.

As part of the ordinary discipline of the Japanese military in that day, each lower rank was physically slapped by those above him. The Japanese officer may have felt that by slapping our shore patrol, the punishment would eventually filter down to the party responsible for beating up their garrison commander. One cannot be sure if this was Japanese military protocol, or simple retribution.

This style of discipline is not part of our American Navy tradition. The guys in the club saw what happened to be an unwarranted Japanese attack on the shore patrol standing in front of the club. They kicked over tables and broke off chair legs, then raced outside to counter the Japanese attack.

Needless to say, we had an international incident at that point.

Five

Last Sea Duty: First Land Duty

Our consulate in Tsingtao was called in to try to appease the Japanese who came out second best in the scuffle. All of our men, not just the instigators, were restricted to shipboard status.

The *Blackhawk* received orders to get under way the next morning, and I was assigned lookout in the crow's nest. I was barely above the fog and could clearly see everything above a two-story level and nothing below that. Mountains of fog in a billowy blanket led out as far as you could see. I was alone, except for an indistinct form that was coming into the bay from the sea.

I saw the main mast of a destroyer slicing through the fog. It was the Japanese! I relayed the information to the officer of the day on the bridge, and he in turn relayed it to the Captain, who maintained his course.

We were there by ourselves with limited firepower on board. We had no American destroyers around to help us. This old AD-9 had one six-inch gun forward and another one aft, no real match for a Japanese destroyer. My sighting was a new development in the incident—the Japanese army had called in their navy.

Due to the fog, the only thing I could see was their ship's masthead with my counterpart in their crow's nest. Radar was not aboard either ship. I can safely say I clearly saw an international incident resolved when that Japanese destroyer glided past us to port as we headed out to sea. They didn't try to stop us. This was July of 1940, the first incident where we had personally come to blows with the Japanese. All hands were aware of the unprovoked sinking by the Japanese of the USS *Panay* a few years before.

After our early departure from Tsingtao, we navigated up the Yangtze River and arrived at Shanghai. Our arrival was impressive because we had a color guard with the ship's band on the quarter deck.

On the usual military post or base, the color guard is there when they raise the flag in the morning and lower the colors in the evening. Aboard our ship, we had a color guard and band on deck, which displayed courtesy bordering on pageantry. When our ship passed the man-of-war of another nation, our band played their national anthem while the color guard saluted them. Like a battle in music to honor each other, they, in turn, played our national anthem and returned the salute.

When all this was taking place I was a yeoman striker in the office on the quarter deck, the perfect location to see everything. The office was known as ComDesRon29. Commander Destroyer Squadron 29. The officer in charge was a Commodore Wiley, who several years before had gone down with the crash of a U.S. Navy zeppelin, but had been rescued by a coxswain, now a petty officer on the *Blackhawk*. They were great buddies with a good working relationship.

Our band had faced the starboard side and played the Japanese national anthem as we passed their ship. Then the band ran over to the port side to play the Australian National Anthem. The military custom of the day was to show respect for the nation represented by a warship in port by playing its national anthem in passing a docked ship, or rendering the anthem of a passing ship in port. They polished it off with the Italian national anthem as we entered Shanghai harbor. I have always wondered how the band learned all those songs—they were so unique.

We sailed up the river playing "Deutschland Über Alles" for a German ship and then segued to "God Save the Queen" for the British ship on the other side; all this in the crescendo and fade of "The Star Spangled Banner" drifting in from from them, though I was convinced we had played "My Country 'Tis of Thee" for the Brits.

Even though the British and Germans were battling each other on the other side of the world, this was a "free port." The sailors were under orders to be peaceful to each other.

We tied up in Shanghai, and liberty was granted, so I went ashore. I was getting to be a rather old salty dog by then. I had seen everything you could see in China, or so I thought. Liberty was longer here; we could stay till midnight. If you had family here or were one of the guys whose wife came over from Manila, you were granted overnight liberty.

The exchange rate at Shanghai was a mere 12:1: a lot less than the favorable Chefoo rates of 20:1. The old hands were aware of this and had already exchanged their gold at the higher Chefoo rate. We had some guys running a money exchange aboard ship, a de facto increase in their pay.

The earth-shattering sight of seeing the Chinese dead lying in the streets and sidewalks in Shanghai convinced me I was not the "old salt" I thought I was. Each morning, a couple of Chinese men would come along and toss the bodies of the old and sick who had starved to death overnight on the "corpse wagon," which took them away for disposal. It was sad to see these unloved people cast aside. The kid-in-the-street stuff went on. The same old "Joe, you likee my sister—" Prostitution was flourishing. In Shanghai, the U.S. Navy did not have direct VD control, like in Chefoo. Sailors did as they pleased here, and social disease came when it pleased.

One night, we were drinking and dancing with some bar girls, and some Italian sailors came in and started fooling around with the girls already claimed by our guys for dancing. Their attempts to lure girls away made our sailors mad. The Americans jumped up and clobbered the Italians. There was another big incident about that brawl. Our sailors' defense reasoning before the captain—"Sir, why the big deal? We didn't involve any *Japanese.*"

After a few days in Shanghai, our ship returned to the Philippines. We went to Cebu and Mindanao, where they grow a lot of papayas and mangos.

We took a sight-seeing tour at the coconut factory in Zamboanga. Carts laden with coconuts were pulled by water buffalos. The off-loaded coconuts were carried to this guy who had what looked like an ordinary V-shaped plow point blade mounted inverted in a stump. He would grasp a coconut with both hands and bring it down on that razor-sharp edge, shaving the husk off and not breaking the meat. It was still fully circular and full of milk. This required masterful precision, for the husk-shaver would have lost a hand if he miscalculated.

We saw how the coconut meat was dried and packaged for shipping. The coconut liquid was drained out to make *tuba,* a fermented milk that would knock the top of your head off. You'd go chasing cars with the local dogs after a few shots of *Tuba.* Samples of liquor were not offered, but we ate all the fresh coconut meat we wanted off the conveyer belt.

I had eaten coconut pies at home made from packets of shredded, dried coconut meat. The fresh was ten times better. Unbelievably better. Back home in Texas, I always had a two-pieces-of-pie limit, but pie was all you could eat there in Zamboanga. I was a kid in a candy factory with no parent in sight. My pig-out that day was the last time in my life I ever ate anything with coconut in it.

While we were shipboard one day and anchored near Cebu, the city and its golf course were victims of a decapitation raid by the Moros, a Muslim group in the south Philippines. This fundamentalist group, fighting Christians as though it were still Crusades times, usually confined its raids to the marketplaces, but this was brazen. From the hundred-year-old constabulary fort, the Philippine police fired on the men swinging chrisses and crumpled men atop their long bolo knives. Moros slaughtered any Christians in their path, but they never hurt a single sailor. Maybe they didn't think of us as Christians.

In the fall of 1940, the USS *Blackhawk* anchored two miles offshore of the equatorial Subic Bay Islands, and stayed moored for six weeks. Surrounded by light blue, clear water, the islands had white, sandy beaches and coconut palms. Our vintage four-stacker World War I destroyers would come in and tie up alongside of our floating machine shop for repair work before going out for naval maneuvers.

Anchored at sea, we had no liberty, but once a week the guys would go swimming off the stern of the ship, using motor launch booms for diving in the ocean. I had seen the big hammerhead sharks that often circled the stern. Though I was a swimmer by then, I said, " 'No way, José am I going to dive off in that drink. Hah!"

All of a sudden we had a big outbreak of gonorrhea on the ship. Impossible. We had no liberty for the past five weeks. Our ancient squadron medical officer, a full commander pushing fifty-five, was complaining about this situation because the commodore was raising hell. A secret guard detail was set up to discover what was going on.

We found out how the epidemic happened. Natives would paddle out at night in *bancas,* small boats with outriggers on them, and tie up to the stern of the ship near the slop chute. The sailors would lower themselves overboard by using a david, the inverted "J" fixture with a block and tackle for lowering life boats. They would have sex with the native girls, then get hauled back up.

One night the ship's unit searchlights were aimed toward the floating bordellos. When word was given, *click!* Flash on. Shine! Twenty sailors got caught in all phases of hugging, humping, and hoisting. They restricted all twenty to the ship.

Back then, a sailor having any venereal disease had to stay aboard ship. Those on the "Restricted List" were mustered twice a day to be certain they were shipboard. On the quarter-deck their names were called out and they responded, "Here," the high point of their life for the next six months. In addition, all the VD sick time was counted as misconduct and had to be made up at the end of their enlistment.

At one stop in Mindanao, we took a bus tour out to visit a native village, returning down the river by riding *bancas.* The natives did all the rowing and guiding on those fast-flowing rapids and tricky currents between the mountains. Though it was a hard ride for me, the natives paddled between those rocks without a scratch, like they had done it every day of their lives.

Using these same bancas, the natives would bring fresh fruit out to the ship. We could buy "lady finger" bananas by the stalk, green, small, with the diameter of a quarter. Despite the green peeling, they were sweet as sugar.

The sales personnel were unbelievable, very attractive young ladies in their teens, curved where they were supposed to be. They wore sarongs from below the belly button to their ankles, leaving the tops completely bare. Like a *National Geographic* come to life, their perky breasts bobbled and rolled with each bounce of ocean waves on the *banca.*

Tan, unblemished skin, sparkling brown eyes, and glistening black hair graced the fairest of faces above slender necks and other charms. But when they parted their pretty lips to smile, I was shocked. No teeth.

I looked again. Black teeth. These lovely fruit vendors were betel nut chewers, their teeth stained by this climbing pepper used as a stimulant by the natives. Chewing betel nut leaves was as much a part of their lives as drinking coffee was to the sailors. This exotic vision of beauty was best when the girls kept their mouths shut.

We paid fifty cents for a whole stalk of the bananas and had one hanging in our office all the time. For fifty cents a dozen they sold mangos so juicy you had to peel them over a wastepaper can. You needed a bath towel nearby to catch the splatter as you ate them.

Between April 1940 and June 1941, my world was simple and carefree. This was the peaceful side of the planet as far as we were concerned. There were "free ports" where belligerents respected each other and gave homage to one another's flag. Our battles were minor bar brawls fought to impress the local girls. I lived an idyllic life and got to see exotic places, and different customs that most people my age had never seen. Japan's superior strength was being whittled down by frequent attacks on their long supply lines, and their expansion into the vastness of China seemed as doomed as Napoleon's venture into Russia.

I experienced an uncomplicated peaceful world in that time, following orders and being an efficient cog in the naval machine. Some world governments were mutually belligerent outside the free ports, and America seemed to be in the world but not of the world. Our portion of this planet found

Americans at peace. Being nonpolitical, I may not have understood the undercurrents. On the surface, I experienced an adult version of my seemingly uncomplicated early childhood.

In an era when a married woman was not allowed to work because a woman's "duty" was to be a homemaker and child-rearer, my mother clerked at Schudee Brothers Clothing Store in downtown Houston to support me and my newly acquired stepfather. She kept their marriage secret from her employer. My stepfather thrived on the hard work and long hours of college but brought some of that dental-school discipline home to apply on his family.

William M. Hill, D.D.S., developed a thriving dental practice, and by the late twenties, we had moved to Houston Heights, a former independent city two miles northwest of Houston. Built in 1891 as a small subdivision of waffle-grid design, Houston Heights had college-named streets crossing numbered avenues. Victorian homes on Heights Boulevard flanking streetcar tracks beside a wide esplanade gave way to bungalows on blocks and brick homes on slabs. The area supported a single-street business district of one- and two-story shops on 19th Avenue, and had its own wave-your-handkerchief two-bench depot at the Katy passenger train stop on 7th Avenue.

My mother and stepfather paid $3,000 for a two-bedroom brick home at 741 East 16th Street, which is still standing. My mother's dad lived with us when my sister, Doris Marie, was born on December 31, 1928, the day of the big snow. It snows once a decade in Houston, an event almost as memorable as getting a little sister. My grandfather bundled me up in layer after layer of clothing to go to the hospital. I could not move.

My mother fussed at her father about overdressing me, but he didn't remember putting on any of my preceding layers. A white-haired gentleman with a thick handlebar moustache, he sat before our faux fireplace with its open-flame gas heater, chewing and spitting tobacco as though there were real wooden logs and embers to catch it. I wonder if he didn't have Alzheimer's disease before it was known by its eponym.

In my part of the 1940 world, I was a cog in the great machine of the United States Navy. I was not a policy maker, but an order follower. My long-range planning came from the chain of command above; my short-range planning was figuring out how to spend the few hours of liberty I was granted each week.

From my office on the quarter-deck of a destroyer tender, I did my job of transmitting orders. I was a proficient paper pusher, trying to be as error-free as possible. I did not want some poor seaman to sit at a pier as ordered and wonder where his ship might be.

I had come a long way from my start as a swabber and gun loader. I watched all the events going on around me but, like most youngsters, did not have a clear picture of what was really happening in the world. My life had become routine: Duty, chow, bunk-roll on desktop, liberty, letters from home, work and fun with shipmates.

I was ready for some change.

Frank Martin Boyd was one of the first-class yeoman who had been transferred from the USS *Blackhawk* to the Commander-in-Chief's office ashore. He was a sharp individual hailing from the Carolinas. After we returned from our journey south of the Subic Bay Islands, Boyd contacted me and wanted to know if I would like to join the naval command office in Manila.

"You ought to come," he said, "it's really a good life. No restriction on hours of liberty. You live ashore. You eat ashore. Good food all the time."

Being in the Navy on land would be different. I took it.

Six

Where Were You on December 8, 1941! Don't You Mean the 7th?

> The question, "Where were you on December the 7th, 1941?" was a cue card for memory of everyone who was older than five, or whenever childhood memories first begin for a generation of Americans. Decades later they could tell you the events of that day unfaded by time, a capsule of personal history tagged to one world event, the sneak attack on Pearl Harbor, Hawaii.
>
> —General knowledge of American culture

> The "sneak attack by the Japs" is now historically recorded as a "surprise attack by the Japanese."
>
> —General knowledge of revisionist history

In June 1941, I requested and received my transfer to the Commander-in-Chief's office, Asiatic Fleet—CINCAF in Navy jargon. The office was at Pier 7 in Manila in the ten-story Moresman Building on the waterfront of Dewey Boulevard. Our living quarters were a nearby hotel. We ate three meals a day in a Chinese restaurant serving American food. We drew regular pay, as though we were at sea, and all of our food and hotel bills were paid by the Navy.

I was a Seaman First striking for Yeoman Third, waiting to take the test after the first of the year. One of my duties was to plot any obstacles on a large navigational map of the ocean. These seaborne objects reported by the Geodetic Survey were floating hazards, mines, and anything else that might be of interest to our ships. I stood watch on a verbal radio communication system that allowed us to be in contact with Cavite Naval Yard, the Army, the Marines, and any ships in the area. Though verbal radio communication compromised our confidentiality, sometimes expediency took priority over secrecy in dealing with Japanese activity or coordinating our own equipment movement.

I was one of the office file clerks whose duty was to read and file navigational reports and all correspondence between my office and other commands. All U.S. Navy files were assigned a subject code number. To assign the right number, I had to read all messages first. Later, when someone wished to find the files on a certain subject, he would go to the code book and look up the subject number. This uniform filing system permitted the consistent flow of information even with a change of command. I handled most of the written communications between Admiral Hart and General Douglas MacArthur. I had to understand them in order to determine their proper file number.

In June and July of 1941, the U.S. Army was strengthening its troop emplacements in the Philippines with men and equipment arriving via transports from the States after an intermediate stop in Hong Kong for liberty after the long journey. This went from a trickle to a roar by November 1941.

The shore patrol in Hong Kong had years of experience with military men on first liberty after a long sea journey. They understood the difficulties sailors could get into and how to help both the military and civilian population survive. Admiral Hart thought it would be nice to offer the services of our shore patrol to the Army military police. We could go over the ropes with them and use our experience to keep MPs out of hot water with the local police, the Chinese police, and the British military police.

Instead of accepting this offer as genuine, General Douglas MacArthur took offense. He advised the admiral that they were perfectly capable of looking out for their own welfare and did not need Navy help. Period. The tone and style of MacArthur's reply was an obvious put-down and, in effect said, "To hell with you. We can handle our own problems." That was the first time I had seen conflict between our navy and our army.

Our dormitory was a civilian hotel where all of CINCAF's office enlisted staff were bivouacked, with maid service. In the restaurant adjacent to the hotel, we ate three meals a day furnished by the Navy. It was run by a Chinese gentleman who prepared choice American meals for us. We could either order from the menu or have his special for the day. It was quite a feast compared to what was being served on the *Blackhawk*, even though the fiscal year closed with the end of summer. All ships in the Navy operated on this budget idea. What you did not spend by the end of the fiscal year was called "excess." Since you did not need "excess," your budget was cut next year by the amount of the excess. This excess in the food budget had to be spent quickly, even if it meant serving steak three times a day at the end of the fiscal year. Our meals ashore were better than shipboard meals, even at the end of the fiscal year.

Everything was furnished, even the maid service. Shipboard, there had been endless cleaning and swabbing details. On land, we lived like regular human beings. We got up in the morning, worked all day, and had liberty every night. It was a huge step up from being shipboard and rolling up your mattress off your desk each morning. You had a bed, a real bed that you could even share if you so desired.

"*Balut! Balut!*" I was awakened by these words many mornings. In Manila, the vendors pushed their two-wheeled wooden carts through the streets peddling *balut,* a Philippine delicacy. This product was prepared by selecting special duck eggs that were about to hatch and soaking them in brine for about a month. These eggs were eaten by breaking the top off one end of the shell and sucking out the rotten-smelling contents. This consisted of juice and the embryonic feathers, beaks, and claws. It still gags me now to think about it. To me it was a fermented rotten egg; to them it was a traditional treat.

One morning the street cries were twice as numerous, twice as loud, and twice as furious. They were a crescendo of "BAL-L-L-L-U-U-U-T! BAL-L-L-U-U-U-T!" but there was something different about sound this morning as I fought off sleep.

"*Balut!*" sounded more like "bomb" or "bombs."

"*Balut! Balut!*" sounded more like "Honolulu."

As wakefulness chased off slumber, I realized that a paper peddler was yelling about an extra edition for December 8th. It was five-thirty in the morning on a Monday. Not a good way to start off a work week.

"Boy, I need a paper," I called out after jumping out of bed.

He folded one up and tossed it to the balcony window. I dropped down a coin.

HONOLULU BOMBED BY JAPANESE read the headline. I could not believe it.

There is a six-hour difference between Hawaii and the Philippines, and because of the international date line, Manila is a day ahead. December 8 in Manila was December 7 in the United States. December 7, 1941—Pearl Harbor Day.

We had fully expected a confrontation with the Japanese, for both nations had been waving the flag at each other. We thought we were ready, but nothing had prepared us for the severity of that first bombing attack on Honolulu. The official reports confirmed the tragic details: Vice-Admiral Chuichi Nagumo of the Japanese Imperial Navy had led a thirty-three-ship striking force to a position two hundred miles north of our Pacific Command Base at Pearl Harbor, Hawaii. Under the cover of darkness, three hundred and sixty Japanese planes took off from his carriers and launched their attack at 7:55 A.M. When the chaos had ended, the Americans had lost eighteen ships, one hundred and seventy-four planes, and three thousand five hundred eighty-one lives. We immediately ceased our routine duties and went into "Operation Wartime," setting round-the-clock watches at the Commander-in-Chief's office.

With the bombing of Pearl Harbor, these Japanese citizens of Japan became "Japs" in our everyday speech and thought patterns. Whether by shorthand speech or derision, the term used for the duration of the war for these Oriental people was "Jap." They were thought of as being short of anything good in their national identity or culture. Human qualities; they lacked in these. Japs, only "Japs" were these Japanese. That's what we called them during the war; and until humane qualities returned, that's what they remained.

The Jap forces were landing on north Luzon shortly after the attack on Pearl Harbor. Between these beaches and the city of Manila were high mountains and narrow, unpaved secondary roads. The mountains rose above the tree line and were impassable for the artillery being off-loaded. After a mountain climb, the Jap infantry could meet ours on the south side of the mountain, but ours would be supplemented with tanks and howitzers.

The U.S. Navy wanted to send in some submarines to attack the Jap troop ships coming into harbor. General MacArthur outranked Admiral Hart by a couple of stars, and military protocol placed the highest ranking officer of dissimilar services in command in an emergency such as this. General MacArthur gave the orders not to torpedo them but to let their troops land. "Then we shall annihilate them," he added.

On that first fateful day, December 8th, the U.S. Army Air Corps had B-17s at Clark Field. A verbal response to questions about the war given to Admiral Hart's command by General MacArthur's command was, "We shall not bomb them until we have been bombed." This response policy for the military operation in the Philippines overlooked the bombing that had already occurred in Hawaii.

That Monday morning a squadron of B-17s took off from Clark Field and flew out over the islands, as they had done regularly for months. Civilians and spies alike knew they carried no bombs on these "training missions," because bombers cannot land loaded. They flew over their prescribed areas and landed back at Clark Field. After parking their planes wing tip to wing tip, the crew then went to the nearest mess hall for their usual noon meal.

As they were chowing down, a squadron of Jap zeroes accompanied by heavy bombers strafed and bombed the B-17s in a precise military line. Before dessert could be started, two-thirds of their planes were burning and the airfield destroyed.

This all took place approximately four hours after the attack on Pearl Harbor. One might attribute "perfect timing" to an attack after a flight lands and parks, but this was not the case. The original Japanese battle plan had been delayed by a heavy ground fog in Formosa that morning.

In Manila, at the CINCAF office in the Morsmund Building, we were advised of the attack on Clark Field and that the city itself would be next. The air raid alert sounded, which indicated the enemy planes had been sighted. As I was the last one to clear out, I glanced over into the admiral's office, which was separated from the rest of the office by a partition. Behind the glass and wood, the admiral was sitting at his desk.

"Admiral Hart, aren't you going down to take cover?" I asked.

"Yes, Kidd, I'll be there in a minute."

He grabbed some papers and came down the hall, where I held the elevator for him. Shortly after we had taken cover in an inside hallway on the first floor, the bombs hit. There was no bomb shelter or basement, and fortunately our building did not take a direct hit.

We went back upstairs to the office and manned our radios. In Admiral Hart's office, glass was everywhere. The concussion from a nearby explosion had turned his window into glass shards that were imbedded in the wall and floor. Had he remained there, he would have been slashed into ribbons of flesh. Here was my initiation into the war.

Everett Jones was a member of the U.S. Army and stationed at Clark Field when the attack turned their new B-17s into junk. He reflected to me that it was now impossible to carry out the MacArthur directive—"We shall not bomb them until they have bombed us"—for we had nothing left to bomb them with.

Clark Field had numerous groups for fighter and bomber squadrons: Pilots, flight crew, ground personnel. Many of these men had arrived before their planes and equipment. Suddenly in the position of not having any planes to fly or service, they were issued rifles and became infantrymen. They had no training in ground warfare, but, after all, "Help was on the way." This knowledge was comforting upon evacuation and withdrawal into Bataan. No one knew that the convoys bringing more planes and equipment had been diverted to Australia, and never reached their original destination of the Philippines.

Being a yeoman in the CINCAF office in Manila during these events, I saw the various reports as they came in and had firsthand knowledge of others. Admiral Hart did not talk to anybody lower than General MacArthur, who had been designated Supreme Commander-in-Chief in the Asiatic area.

On December 10, 1941, we were advised that the enemy airplanes were approaching the Manila area. The Japs were flying higher than our capabilities of reaching them with our three- and five-inch antiaircraft batteries. The fuses on our projectiles would explode before they got to the altitude of the enemy, giving their planes but a harmless puff of wind.

We watched the Jap planes come over and bomb at will. Our antiaircraft shots exploded far below the beautiful "V"-formation of their twenty-seven heavy bombers. They passed over Manila and went ten miles out beyond Cavite Navy Yard. Then they crisply broke into three groups of nine planes, made a one-hundred-and-eighty-degree turn, and reapproached Manila Bay.

The pilots, knowing they were safe from our antiaircraft, did not deviate or even budge. They flew on a specific course and bombed the Cavite Navy Yard, totally destroying it. Many men were killed, and our ships were severely damaged. The USS *Tannenger*, a minesweeper moored to Machina Wharf, was hit by the bombers but managed to escape the ensuing holocaust. At Pier 18, the USS *Perry*, and the USS *Pillsbury*, two destroyers from my former outfit ComDesRon-29, sustained damages.

The wounded at Cavite Navy Yard were transported by ambulance from their injury point to the docks. Here fifty-foot motor launches carried them on a half-hour trip from across the bay to a civilian dock off Dewey Blvd. in Manila.

Getting ground transportation from dock to civilian hospital fell to our CINCAF office in Manila. We were told, "Go down and commandeer any civilian transportation you can find. Trucks, cars, anything. Issue a receipt for the vehicle and proceed to the pier where these motor launches will be landing." We assisted in unloading the wounded and transporting them to the civilian hospital.

I distinctly remember giving a man a receipt for a brand-new four-door Ford sedan. By the end of that day the seats, headliner and upholstery were trashed from blood stains from the wounded. I have often wondered if the owner ever got reimbursed.

The duty uniforms of the day for CINCAF personnel consisted of white uniforms, black shoes, black neckerchiefs and white hats. Since the dock area was totally crimson from the blood of injured men, our uniforms changed from white to pink to red as we helped those guys into the commandeered vehicles. Sticky handprints were everywhere as we raced to get them to the hospitals. I never knew what happened to those wounded men, whether they were later evacuated from the hospital or got captured by the Japs. That was the most eye-opening experience of my young life up to that time.

General MacArthur declared Manila an open city on December 25th, hoping that the Japanese would spare the civilian population from further bombing, and that tactic seemed to help.

My rude awakening continued. On December 25th, we received the order that we were to give up our positions in Manila and surrounding Luzon and withdraw to Corregidor and the Bataan peninsula. After all, "Help was on the way," so "Merry Christmas."

Admiral Hart and the CINCAF office were sent to the safety of Monkey Point Tunnel on Corregidor. I was the junior man in the office, and since everybody, including the clean-up crew, was senior to me, I was designated to go to the Marvales Section Base in Bataan. It was three miles across the bay from Corregidor and south of the front lines.

I left Manila aboard a PT boat, perhaps the same one that General MacArthur later rode out on, and was its only passenger. An hour-and-fifteen-minute ride in broad daylight carried me thirty miles across the open Manila Bay, a tempting strafing target for any Jap plane, but there was none.

I felt important on this trip. Anybody doing anything with what he had to fight the Japs felt important. In the haste to destroy anything helpful to the enemy, the luxury of a written order was absurd. I had verbal orders only: To be available to Commander Cheek of Naval Intelligence at Monkey Point on Corregidor Island. I was to be his driver when he made his inspection trips to Bataan. Perhaps I would be vital in the transmission of orders when the help on the way arrived at Bataan.

Whatever self-importance I may have conjured up was quickly dissolved when the PT pulled to a bombed-out dock at Marvales. All around me were blown-apart buildings lying on the ground, a redestruction of previously bombed targets still afire. I saw no one for me to meet, not even someone in a naval uniform.

I asked a lieutenant on the PT boat what his feeling of my situation was.

"Find somebody to report to," he said.

The roar of his engines and splash of his wake drowned out my feeble "Who?"

I walked ashore, into the war, and all I had was a .45 pistol, a field helmet, and a change of clothing. I started looking around for someone to report to and for something to eat. I soon discovered that neither were to be found. I was Seaman First Class Kidd, Darwin F., a yeoman, without written orders, trained in proper office procedures, and I had no senior officer to report to. There were no barracks or tents. As far as camping out and dealing with the many problems confronting our forces in the field, I had no training. I began to wonder, *Where do they want me now? Do they even want me? Am I expendable?* It was not easy being the junior man.

The USS *Canopus*, a sub tender, was camouflaged and moored to the side of a mountain that reached the water's edge. This floating machine-shop was never seen by the Jap planes and afforded repairs to the submarines we had coming in and out of the blockaded Manila Bay. The fire power of our ships was no match for the Jap flotilla of men-of-war. Fortunately, the undersea attacking power of the Japanese Navy did not match their surface power, and our submarines could go back and forth across the Manila Bay entrance at night.

I finally found the Manila shore patrol unit bivouacking in a storm drain. This culvert underneath the road circled around the bay side of the mountain near the USS *Canopus*.

The shore patrol detachment was composed of a Chief Petty Officer and seven sailors. They were looking for proper naval authorities to report to themselves, but they were the only thing naval ashore.

"Throw your gear down and make yourself at home," said the chief.

Everything was total chaos. All the buildings were bombed and blown apart, so there was no place to eat or sleep. Nothing but bewildered people. Desolate as it was, that culvert was our only protection during air raids.

One Jap dive bomber made a run on us, looking back as his five-hundred-pounder fell toward us and the culvert. He failed to pull his plane up quickly enough and flew into the side of the mountain. We were taking cover and joked about claiming him as one plane shot down.

His bomb fell short of whatever the target, our trucks on the gravel road above or us and the culvert, and hit a hundred feet away from our crude bomb shelter. In a wet area, rather than the gravel, it dug a crater thirty feet across. Heaven knows how deep the crater was, because it filled with greenish water that smelled like gunpowder. We were shaken up, but nobody had gotten hurt. His miss was taken as a special present, our Merry Christmas in 1941 on Bataan.

Bivouacking out in the middle of a jungle was certainly radical change from what my army uncle had told me I should experience in the Navy during wartime. At night, the monkeys in the trees were throwing stones at us. During the day, we were trying to shoot the monkeys for something to eat.

A displaced little lieutenant chanced upon our motley crew and, due to rules of rank, came to be in charge. Unlike our seasoned chief, this full lieutenant was quick to have you volunteer for dangerous and useless tasks.

We had tried on numerous occasions to assist the Army, and it was a foregone conclusion that we needed to have some food first. But for burnt monkey parts, our last meal was three days before. We were unable to get supplies from the *Canopus.* The lieutenant assessed the situation: No food here. Starvation. Battle lines to the north unknown, possible death or capture by Japanese. What unit of whose army was fighting where was totally unknown to us. Probably unknown to the opposing army units. "Help was on the way," but right then we needed to have *food* on the way.

He asked for volunteers, two days before New Year's, 1942, to take our three gray USN-identified two-ton stake trucks to Manila and get food and supplies from the Navy's cold storage.

I had not eaten in three or four days and was hungry enough to volunteer for anything. I knew how to drive a stick shift truck and double clutch. Two other hungry guys also volunteered.

Before our mission, the lieutenant gave us a briefing, "You realize that the city itself has been declared an 'open city.' When you get there, you are going to have checkpoints. You will not be allowed to carry your rifles and sidearms into the open city. You will have to check all your firearms at the sentry post with the guard on duty. You men understand that?"

We said nothing, and the lieutenant walked off.

Seven

On Bataan

"Help is on the way." This statement of comfort, given us at the beginning of hostilities, contrasts with:

We're the battling bastards of Bataan,
No mamma, no papa, no Uncle Sam,
No aunts, no nephews, no nieces,
No pills, no planes, no artillery pieces,
And nobody gives a damn.

This poem turned up on the front line. The author was Frank Hewlett, a war correspondent with UPI (United Press International); he spent a lot of time with the men up front.

I thought, *Boy, it doesn't make sense to check your weapons with a stranger in time of war.* The enemy, as far as I knew, was coming down toward Manila. Hell, there were Japs out there! I turned to the other guys and said, "Are you going to turn in your weapon?"

"Hell no!" They laughed. "Who would turn in their weapons when you're coming back to where you have to use them? Who would leave 'em there while some other turkey abandons the guardhouse, if there is such a place, and your weapons would no longer be available? Don't turn them in."

"We won't turn them in."

"Okay."

We took off at night because the Japs had control of the air space and a moving vehicle invited strafing. Our trip started on Highway 110, which ran through the jungle and coastline. We kept our lights off to preserve secrecy and were unsure of who else was moving on the road. The Japs controlled all of northern Luzon, and were fast closing in on Manila.

At one point the two-lane road became a one-way bridge over some mountain stream splashing seaward in the darkness. I was third in line and was coming off the bridge, when something moving and metallic clipped the last three feet of my truck bed. I thought the Japs had caught me. After knocking off a chunk of the truck and bending the bed, whatever it was kept on going. I assumed it was an American tank also running without lights. Infrared lights, standard in night tank maneuvers years later, were not utilized at this point.

We continued, but I thought I needed to change my britches. How many more tanks and one-way bridges lay ahead? I had never been on this road in my life. I didn't know where I was going. I was following those other guys in trucks who didn't know where they were going either. Fair enough.

The driver ahead produced a map. The crunch of gravel of Highway 110 became the crunch of gravel of Highway 7 to San Fernando. At sunrise, we were rolling over the pebbles of Highway 3 into Manila. It was New Year's Eve, 1942.

We went down to the Navy cold storage and told them, "Fill 'em up."

"Be back at 1600 hours for departure," they answered.

We left the trucks there and I went over to see my girlfriend, who was a Mestiza, part Filipino and part Australian. I talked to her alone for a while and we realized that we would never see one another again, the reality being hammered home by each news flash of the Japs' nearness. I talked to her and her family, but radio reports that the Japs were just outside the city limits made us rush back to the Navy cold storage at one-thirty in the afternoon. The damn Japs were entering the city. We could not wait for darkness; we had to get the hell out of there.

We made our minds up that if we encountered Japs anywhere, we would abandon the loads, pour gas on them and set them afire. We would go to the beach, get some bancas, and paddle our way to Marvales.

We were on the run, and those trucks were so heavily overloaded that when we would hit a bump the axles would hit bottom. There was little arch left in those 1940s-style leaf springs. Almost inverted, they let the bed get sanded by the tires.

At one corner in suburban Manila we heard gunfire and saw people running every which way. Coming down one cross-street toward us were armed men in Jap Army uniforms. They were only half a block away, but they were too involved with civilians on the sidewalks to pay attention to three distant gray trucks.

At another point, we were driving parallel to advancing Japs one block over. There was a lot of gunfire, but none of it hit our trucks. Maybe they were sticking to a precise battle plan that scheduled a sweep on that street and not ours. Those were our closest calls in Manila.

We were soon on our way to San Fernando again, then the northernmost position of our troops that had evacuated to the Bataan Peninsula. We noticed some tanks up on the hillside firing at us and the surrounding area. We were burning up our tires to stay ahead of them, and we succeeded. Outside San Fernando at some nameless river, an MP was motioning to us.

"Hurry! Get across the river," he yelled while he took cover from incoming shells. Our lead truck stopped and wanted to know if it was safe for us to go across the bridge.

"If you don't go right away," yelled the MP, "you won't get across. We're gonna blow it up."

We crossed. They did—*someone* did. The bridge collapsed. Whether it was the handiwork of our own engineers or direct hits from Jap tanks, that bridge collapsed into the river.

We pulled into San Fernando at sundown and felt protected by the approaching darkness. The city had been bombed. In the railyard, an ammunition train headed for positions in the Bataan peninsula was now burning and exploding. The blazing glare from the fires was so bright you could have read a newspaper by it.

With the bridge on the other side blown away and American troops between us and the Japs, we figured we were safe for the moment. We stopped and had ourselves some supper: sardines, canned salmon and a loaf of bread. After our meal, we got back into our trucks and headed south back into the Bataan peninsula. The rest of our trip back to Marvales was uneventful. Since our cargo was a lot of canned food and fruit, we were eating pretty well. Compared to gnawing tough monkey meat a few days before, it was excellent.

Looking back in later years, I thought how dumb I was to volunteer for that detail and how lucky I was to get out of Manila alive. We were practically rubbing elbows with the Japs. We went right by them and made it. It was sure stupid luck. Nothing else to it. No brilliant maneuvers. It was luck and stupidity that got us through.

MacArthur commanded, but chaos ruled. We were one of the many points of origin for the new American slang word: snafu, an acronym for Situation Normal, All F——d Up. *Fouled up*, of course.

Unsettlement began with the most basic of our needs, which were now handled in a new way. Food: After starvation, it was plentiful until the three truckloads of it ran out. We shared with others in the immediate area. Shelter: bivouac area in a culvert. Water: from black rubber field bags or the occasional mountain stream, but we were in the dry season. Bathing: Manila Bay, shore line. Salt water only. No soap. Watch out for a Jap plane on a sortie. There were not too many baths taken. Salt water is hard on your skin. Fresh water would be available when the wet season made the streams swell again; but then our bivouac in the culvert would be flooded. Lights: the sun during the day and at night we had the chance to see the magnificent Milky Way, illuminating little in our muddle.

Dental hygiene came via cutting off a twig, stripping its bark, and cutting one end crossways a few times so that it could be chewed on and made to bristle like an artist's brush. Saliva or water made "toothpaste."

Latrine a-la-leaf became the number-one splashing sport until favorite wet leaves turned from greens to yellows and the ground reeked from urinating fellows. As a land "head" for number two, defecation was accomplished behind the bush with your feet very wide apart. This stance lessened the necessity for using foliage as toilet tissue. The jungle was big enough to handle our situation, but with the supplies as part of the help on the way, these minor aggravations would be alleviated. So we reasoned.

Chaos continued with communications. Very little of it occurred between the command post and disparate field units. I made three reporting trips by PT boat from Marvales to Commander Cheek on Corregidor Island. I was on one of these trips when we heard by radio broadcast of the April

18, 1942 daylight raid on Tokyo by Colonel James Doolittle's B-25s. It was a morale booster, to think that we had hit the enemy in his capital city. I brought this news back to our group on Bataan.

As we made another trip from Bataan to Corregidor, I took a short cut to the navy tunnel by traveling through Malinta Tunnel. Many side tunnels came off the main tunnel at angles, and I got lost in one of the lateral hallways. I entered a dark room, where I waded through a lot of paper trash that covered the floors. I looked closer and saw that the "trash" was money, singles, fives, tens, twenties, and even fifties, all cut in half. I spotted some mutilated hundred-dollar bills and bags of silver dollars from Manila's banks. Later on, I heard that the silver was dropped off the north pier into a deep part of the bay. I definitely did not belong in this place. So I located the exit and departed from the army's safe outpost.

Instead of hauling Commander Cheek by car on Bataan, I hauled U.S. Army guys to front-line positions in one of our grey trucks with USN emblazoned on its cab door. Chaos. We managed to transport quite a few Army troops and some pilots without planes who were now infantrymen from point "A" to point "B" on Bataan. I took one load of soldiers up on a new mountain road recently made by an army bull-dozer. It was little more than a trail of pushed-over trees and bare earth. The truck, geared in grandma and standing room only in the back, ground to a stall halfway up, when the lieutenant in charge said, "This will do. We'll get out now."

The road was too steep to merely back it down at the beck and call of gravity, so the lieutenant assisted me in turning the truck around. I went back down without getting strafed or bombed, for a Japanese plane would strafe a single man if it saw him. We stayed out of sight and operated mostly at night.

After arriving in Marvales on December 25th, I made several trips to Corregidor to check in on the Navy Intelligence tunnel. In February 1942, we approached Corregidor and landed in the dock area, located on "bottom side." The shortest route to our CINCAF Offices at the Monkey Point location was to go though Malinta Tunnel, the Army tunnel on Corregidor. As I was exiting the south end of that highly protected, magnificent structure one day, I heard the air-raid alert going off. I was walking around and in between all the sandbags placed at the opening of the tunnel, when this tall individual comes charging into the entranceway, knocking me down. From my position on the ground, I hollered, "Watch where you're going!"

Tall never looked back or slowed his step. He disappeared around a left angle bend in the trench of sandbags and headed for the tunnel. Another officer following this particular gentleman reached down and helped me back to my feet.

I said, "Who in the hell was that *sonofabitch*?" I looked on the tan shirt collar of my uniformed helper and saw an eagle flying there, denoting an army colonel. Uh-oh.

"You don't know who that was?" The colonel was aghast.

"Absolutely not."

"That's General MacArthur."

"Well, he sure was in one helluva big hurry."

"Yes, he was," said the colonel.

That was the only time I ever got close enough to MacArthur to know for sure he was even on the island. I still feel he should have looked where he was going. I thought to myself, *He sure is scared of air-raid alerts.* I guess that's why he was called "Dugout Doug."

Air-raid alerts were sounding all the time. Not each one was accompanied by an attack on your part of the island.

Those who were assigned places in the tunnels as permanent residents felt safe in their shelter and preferred it to the uncertainty of the outside. Some "tunnel rats" feared *ever* going outside.

For those not assigned a permanent tunnel, the air-raid alerts were not so disturbing. We figured the Japs had more important targets than some lone GI behind a tree or in a ditch. It was not bravado on our part; being outside was simply our way of life. We were too busy to think about the daily air raids.

In March, I went back through Malinta Tunnel on my way to our CINCAF office in Corregidor. Fortunately, I got through the shortcut without being run over by our glorious leader. Upon my return from Monkey Point, I decided to visit Queens' Tunnel, where all the other Navy personnel were housed. I was walking the mountain road on the Queens Tunnel side of Corregidor, when I noticed two naval officers approaching on the gravel road. Thinking they were on their afternoon stroll, I kept on approaching them.

As we got closer, I recognized Captain Rockwell, the captain of the USS *Nevada* when I was an in turret number one. He was the officer who authorized my transfer to the Orient. That Sunday morning in his private quarters was the turning point in my life. You bet I recognized him, and now he was an admiral.

I saluted and spoke to him, "Afternoon, sir." I was Navy-wise enough now to know the man of lower rank gives a courteous greeting, but does not initiate conversation with the man of higher rank.

"Hold it just a minute, son," he said, returning my salute. "Your name is Kidd, isn't it?"

"Yes, sir." I was very surprised that he knew who I was.

"Well, how do you like your tour of duty? I'll bet you'd like to be back on the *Nevada.*" He chuckled.

"I don't know about the *Nevada*," I replied, "but I would like to be back in the United States, sir." I smiled. "All joking aside, I have enjoyed the tour until now. I wish to congratulate you on your promotion to admiral."

"Well, thank you, son. You take care of yourself and, most of all, your health. Bye."

"Thank you, admiral," I said as I continued my walk to the dock for my return to Bataan.

We had tried to use some grenades to dynamite for fresh fish down at the wharf of the Marvales section base. We pulled pins, dropped them over, and expected them to go off. Most of them were duds. Only one of five of those World War I grenades would go off, but when they did, plenty of fish floated to the surface. It was a very effective way to get food. I can't say that in the future it did much for nature around us, but, in war, environmental concerns fifty years hence were not our concern. Although there were no natives around when we fished in this manner, I have wondered more than once if the Filipinos might have seen some of our GIs effectively fish, and copied it to being a national disgrace today.

All of our equipment was old. It was pathetic, like Springfield rifles, the World War I, bolt-action rifles. I got hold of a BAR (Browning Automatic Rifle), that I kept hidden in the truck because it was too heavy to carry around. I carried a Springfield rifle and a bandolier of thirty-ought-six and two extra clips of .45 ammunition.

We decided to do something about our lack of reliable hand grenades. The Naval section had a mine shaft full of torpedoes, dynamite, and all sorts of ammunition. It was stored back in the gray granite mountain a quarter mile from the harbor where the USS *Canopus* was moored.

A lieutenant at the section base who, in civilian life, had been an engineer taught us how to make our own grenades.

We got a bunch of empty number-two milk cans from the Navy mess hall, cut the tops out, and packed them with bits of steel and chain. Then we cut dynamite sticks in two and packed them inside as well. The dynamite was so old, the nitroglycerine oozed out like teardrops. Because we had no gloves, our bare hands absorbed the nitro, and we got unbelievable headaches. To finish off our grenades, we pushed down a three-inch fuse through the cap and sealed the whole thing with tar.

You had to light a match and toss it. The fuse usually lasted thirty seconds. We did a lot of fishing but never got to use them in combat.

There was nobody in the jungle but the monkeys, us, and the mosquitos. I began having freezing chills that would suddenly change to high fever. This condition left me disoriented, so they dropped me off in a field hospital. The hospital, called "Little Bagio," was a series of tan tents in a green jungle clearing, away from the fighting troops. It was clearly marked as a hospital by the white sheet with a big red cross on its roof. I was sicker than a dog. Diagnosis: malaria. Treatment: They took quinine powder and molded pills out of it. Each one was as big as the end of your little finger and not that easy to swallow. I do not know about the dosage, and I wonder if the doctors were just giving you as much as you could swallow twice a day.

The second day after I had checked in, the Japs bombed the hospital, killed a bunch of patients, and wounded some nurses and doctors. From the ground a falling bomb sounds like someone tearing a bed sheet in two. The red cross clearly marking the hospital had been taken as a bulls-eye by the dive bomber. Was this an accident or a planned violation of the Geneva Convention? I think the latter.

Believe it or not, my record of being interned with malaria in Little Bagio survived the war and got back to the

Navy Department in the United States to become a part of my military records. I have a copy of that entry in my files.

The wounded, some of whom had legs blown off, had been reduced to sleeping on bare boards in the jungle. I figured a fella could get hurt up here. I was safer back in Marvales Bay than here at the hospital. So I grabbed my bag of quinine pills and departed.

In early April of 1942, the big push had started up on the front lines. It was a matter of time before Bataan would fall. The help on the way had better get here, and quick. The Japs were rebombing the remains of what they had already bombed. There was little left of the Marvales section base. All the buildings were blown up or on fire. Maybe a floor would be standing, but nothing would be of any use.

We were within a half mile of where they were bombing. No big deal. There was another fire going on down at Marvales. A nameless little lieutenant jumped up and, in a squeaky nasal voice, said, "All right, men. I want *men*! We gotta go down there and put out the fires."

"Nothing but blown-apart buildings," said a sailor in the crowd. "Let 'em burn."

"Ohhh no. We gotta go down and fight 'em. I want volunteers!"

Not a single man got up. Finally the Chief Petty Officer got up and said, "Lieutenant, sit down!"

He sat back down. On the strength of everything that took place in Bataan and Corregidor, this little lieutenant *recommended himself* for the Navy Cross! The award was denied.

The decision came down that the enemy would be upon us shortly. A detached naval group had orders to scuttle the USS *Canopus* in the deep water where it was moored at the side of the mountain. We were to drive our three trucks off the pier and then seal the entrance to the mountain-side ammo tunnel located midway between the *Canopus* and the last block of the Marvales base at the jungle's edge. Then we could leave to avoid capture.

We did these things in that order. I was on the last detail to seal the tunnel entrance. Our chief had gotten word as to how many boxes of dynamite it would take to seal it, but the dynamite we were using was itself unstable. Those of us who carried it did so carefully, and the nitroglycerine oozed onto our hands as we gently eased the boxes down in a pile for fuse placement. We could hear small arms fire going on outside, but we did not know if it was our guys opposing the enemy, or the Japs overrunning our position.

We rolled the fuse down from the dynamite boxes at the front of this tunnel, but it went only halfway down the slope to our motor launch. The gentle slope from the tunnel turned to a forty-five-degree angle for the last thirty feet. We lit the fuse and ran. We were preparing the motor launch when that sucker blew.

The vibrations from the entrance explosion racked the walls and all that volatile dynamite in back blew up. Those blasts set off the torpedoes and everything else. Boulders the size of small houses blew over us a mile out to sea. None of them hit us, but the concussion knocked us flat. The whole mountainside shifted and started rolling down. We got in that motor launch and hauled out of there.

I do not know if there was anybody on top of the mountain. I have often wondered how many people, if any, we might have killed that day, and if they were American or only Japs. Our intent was to seal the ammunition tunnel, but, instead, we blew up the mountain. It was the biggest Fourth of July in April that I had ever seen.

Eight
Corregidor

Upon arrival at Corregidor, I immediately went out to the Naval Intelligence Tunnel at Monkey Point, where the CINCAF people had moved. Corregidor guards the Manila Bay entrance near the island of Luzon from the South China Sea being in the channel two miles from its province of Bataan, and seven miles from shores of Cavite province. The four-mile-long rocky fortified island of 1735 acres is shaped like a giant tadpole with the tail facing northeast. The head topography rises 628 feet at the apex with two tailward flat plateaus called "top side" and "middle side" to the sandy beach called "bottom side." Topside runs northeast on the body to a second mountain, Malinta Mountain, containing two major tunnels. Near the end of the tadpole tail is Monkey Point where the smallest tunnel runs into a much smaller mountain.

The Top Side batteries of Fort Crockett and Fort Garry were on the south end of the island; between Corregidor and the northern shore of Cavite was a "concrete battleship" called Fort Drum. Originally a small rocky islet, it was fortified with cement and shaped to look like a battleship facing seaward with two massive fourteen-inch twin guns to the bow. At the turn of the century Corregidor, called by many "The Gibraltar of the Pacific," could have turned back any fleet in the world wanting to enter Manila Bay.

In Malinta Mountain was Malinta Tunnel, the army command tunnel built between 1922 and 1932 with finished walls of cement inside. It was so spacious that a streetcar ran through it on a regularly scheduled route. The main tunnel was twenty-four feet wide and eight hundred thirty-six feet long. Being the largest of Corregidor's tunnels, Malinta housed a 1,000-bed U.S. Army hospital and MacArthur's command headquarters, all safely tucked away from the bombing attacks. Its outside entrances were stacked with sandbags crowding the narrow walkways at right angles.

I eventually found the Navy headquarters, CINCAF, located from Manila to a smaller tunnel on "Monkey Point." I greeted our old office force, but there was no room for me in that tunnel. They suggested I go down to Queens Tunnel, also used by the Navy.

I returned to Queens Tunnel, which was adjacent to Malinta Tunnel in the same mountain but not as large or elaborate. My friend Carruthers was assigned there because his ship had been sunk off of Corregidor.

"Aah aah aah," they say, "the tunnel is full. All the survivors off Bataan are assigned to the 4th Marine Naval Reserve Battalion."

"Where the hell do the 4th Marines come in?" I say. "I'm in the Navy."

"It's the naval reserve battalion."

"But I'm on active duty."

"You have been assigned to the 4th Marine Naval Reserve Battalion; you will report to them." All other Navy personnel previously assigned duty stations remained in their respective places of assignment. This was confusing. I felt expendable again.

"Well, who do I report to?" The confusion seemed perpetual.

"You report to Captain Moore, uh, U.S. Army! Up on topside, that's the first big mountain. The batteries were located up there."

I said, "Well, okay." Out of the tunnel, I traipsed up the hillside and located Captain Moore.

"I don't know what I'm doing up here, Captain Moore, sir," I said, initiating a salute. "I'm Navy, and I'm up here to do something, but I don't know what."

"You dig yourself a foxhole, young man," he said. "You might as well start digging it over in the side of the mountain. You dig it big enough so you can get inside and get out of the way of any projectiles that might be coming in from Bataan."

Though there was plenty of coverage with the lush green vegetation, trees, bushes, etc., they were no protection for the concussion of nearby shells hitting. A foxhole in the ground or in the side of a mountain is no protection from a direct hit. Nothing is.

"Ohhhh, okay," I said. With nothing more than a mess kit knife and a mess-kit lid I started digging into the hard-packed clay of the mountainside. Some other guys from Bataan were there, trying to dig with the same equipment. We had no truncheon tools or anything like that, but we pooled our efforts and dug a community foxhole for the four of us. We dug it deep enough so we could crawl in and sit down with six inches to spare over our heads. We had nothing to shore it up with, but when you had carved your way back into hard clay all night long with knives and lids, it did not make any difference. That is where we spent the next few weeks prior to the surrender of Corregidor.

I had a chance in 1978 to return to Corregidor and visit our emergency architectural marvel. I found it surprisingly intact in the mountainside, facing the road overlooking jungle greenery and the blue of the sea.

Between Monkey Point and the rest of the island there was a valley where a 155mm gun emplacement was dug down into the sand. With no protection other than sandbags around it, that gun was manned by Philippine scouts. My position was on the opposite side of the mountain from Marvales Bay. From that position, we had a clear view of the beaches on Bataan where the Japs had set up their artillery. They had moved in heavy equipment from Singapore and everything they had captured from Bataan, and positioned them for better firing angles on Corregidor. I could look from my position on the side of the mountain at the muzzle blasts from the Jap artillery pieces being used to shell us as directed by their spotter balloon.

Corregidor's forts were primarily equipped to fire south toward the sea and were unable to respond to enemy bombardment from Bataan. Much to our dismay, the Japs were in the safe zone since our shore batteries were unable to train and fire in their direction. The Japs were in Bataan firing at our rear continuously every day. I know for a fact that one gun in bottom side, manned by Filipino scouts, could return fire with their single 155mm gun. Since their gun emplacement was in the direct line of fire from the Bataan artilleries, these brave men would fire a single shot, then run for cover when the Jap crews released their barrage. As soon as the Japs ceased their shelling, usually in a couple of hours or so, they would slip out to the sandbagged emplacement and lob another one. It was truly David vs. Goliath, but instead of a slingshot, David had only a spitwad.

Of the several forts located on topside, Fort Gary was located directly above our position, its large gun permanently pointed seaward and now useless for battle. The fort had one four-by-four-foot window in one of the magazines, which was protected only by its position. It was one foot lower than the top of a hill, its unprotected back door facing

Bataan. The incoming shell would have to arc over the hill and drop into the small window from a position miles away. The Japs had an observation balloon up, and their spotters finally got the range on the fort's window in April.

I was half asleep, leaning against the wall in our community foxhole and hearing the varied pitch and loudness of shells going off somewhere on the mountainside, when the concussion wave from an explosion above us roared directly through the mountain clay to us. It slammed my steel helmet onto my head, cutting my scalp. Then a landslide started above us, with debris and shell casings tumbling down on the road in front of our shelter. Day instantly became night as the rubble and dust of the avalanche roared past to the water's edge ten stories below us. I thought the cave would collapse and we would be buried alive. So I followed my impulse to bolt out of the hole.

"Where the hell are you going?" yelled a guy who grabbed my belt and stopped me at the entrance. "You'll get killed out there. That stuff's falling."

Luckily our hole was not covered up, and we crawled out after everything had settled down. People who saw the explosion said that some of the mortars mounted in concrete were blown a mile out to sea. It was difficult to compare this event to the mountaintop we blew up. I did not see this one; I just felt it.

I was one of the fortunate ones who had escaped Bataan with a steel helmet. Some of those guys had nothing but their sailor hats. Those little white Navy hats against the green and brown background made an easy moving target for Jap gunners to hone in on. The sailors soon learned to dye their hats brown with coffee or coffee grounds. It was painfully obvious that our Navy personnel were ill-equipped to fight a ground war against a well-trained enemy.

While sitting in the hole during the shelling, we basically passed the time talking about what we were going to do when the war was over. A rubberized canvas bag of water was brought to us and hung from a tree near our cave. Food came to us by a small go-cart-type vehicle, a three-wheel truck with wheels half the diameter of a regular car. We had half a canteen cup of cracked wheat as a porridge ladled out for us twice a day. One time they got fancy and had ham. One ham for 125 men. My slice was so thin that you could see through it, but it was a tasty little treat. Our general conclusion: We are low on provisions.

Talking and chewing became difficult for me because I had a swollen jaw and pus draining in my mouth. An abscessed wisdom tooth meant I had to go down to Queens' Tunnel to get operated on, a two-mile round-trip in the open, where Jap artillery would open up with multiple pieces on anyone exposed. I took cover and kept well hidden on the way to the dentist. I wasn't a bit worried about the tooth as he pulled it or about the painful abscess. It was the trip back up to my foxhole that concerned me. Evidently the Japs were goofing off. I did not get fired on.

When I got back in my hole, Captain Moore was out in the open talking to Warrant Officer Rearden, a Marine who was with us. The Japs opened fire from Bataan and a piece of shrapnel flew by, missing their heads by six inches. Shueeiip! It was a piece of shell casing. From that point on, they did not stand around gazing into the wild blue yonder toward Bataan.

Shelling by the forces of the Rising Sun became a daily event that lasted from sunrise until sunset. The blasts were intermittent and spasmodic—on the average, about one per second directed to one part of the island or another. They always came to your part, but you never knew when.

We heard the boom of the muzzle fire, seconds later a whooshing sound, and then the *kaboom* of the exploding shell. Whether nearby *boom* or far-off *pop*, it was one per second, though they fired at will. As you got used to the sound, they would suddenly let up at noon for an hour. Hungry us; we knew the Japs had knocked it off for chow.

Then their restart came after they had been filled, and once a second they blasted from different parts of Bataan until 2:30 or 3:00 P.M. Knock it off. Teatime. They rubbed it in that they were all powerful. Once full of tea, they restarted their bombardment until sunset, when they would knock it off for chow and sack time. Then we could risk it outside for personal relief time. We stayed covered, preferring the indoors of the cave to the leafy coverage alongside the road. Our foxhole had no head, so we tried to confine the roadside toilet activities to nightfall. We did not want to get caught with our pants down, literally.

To honor their emperor's birthday the Japs gave us a continuous barrage that started at daylight and did not stop until darkness. It sounded like a bunch of forty-millimeter "pom-pom" guns firing at the same time; only these guns were much larger. The booms and crashes were bigger, but the rhythm was *pom-pom*, like what you hear in the World War II movies when our naval vessels are firing rapidly at enemy aircraft.

At least six per second. All day long. No letup for chow or teatime. They gave up those pleasures to honor their emperor and pound us into submission. It was estimated that the number of projectiles hitting Corregidor that day alone would fill one hundred and twenty-nine boxcars. In more modern-day terms, the saturation of their shelling comes out to be one boxcar of shells fired for each twenty football fields of space, and we were on the fifty-yard line.

There was not a tree or a bush left standing on the entire island after they celebrated the emperor's birthday. Everything was blown apart like it had been run over with a big bulldozer. We sat inside as everything outside went from green to brown.

The realization hit us. There was no help on the way. Nothing official. Just scuttlebutt, but sometimes scuttlebutt is truth. If help was on the way, it was not on the way to us. We learned it had been diverted to Australia. We were expendable. We were forgotten. We were about to be sacrificed by our government, and there was no comfort in learning that our chiefs were safe in Australia with all the food and equipment we desperately needed.

When we got a report at approximately 9:30 P.M. that the Japs had started landing on the north end of Corregidor, between Malinta Tunnel and Monkey Point, where the Naval Intelligence and CINCAF offices were located, Captain Moore's battle cry was, "All right, fall out, men."

So we fell out, meaning we assembled for combat with an assortment of small arms. We were a bunch of sailors, a few Marines and U.S. Army captain. Captain Moore said, "We're gonna march down and go through Malinta Tunnel because we won't be subject to shell fire if we go through the tunnel. Then we'll go out the other side and engage the enemy landing forces."

"Okay," I kept telling myself. "I got in the Navy. What in the hell am I doing here?" Shades of my Uncle Jack's advice, "Go Navy, not Army," floated through my head. His advice was colored by his World War I trench-warfare experience. We were not in trenches, unless you considered foxholes little trenches. Foolish thought. We were going to be out in the open. The attacking enemy would be in the open, maybe.

Malinta Tunnel was strongly defended. The entrances were all sandbagged about three layers thick; it could stop shrapnel from shells or bombs.

We marched into the center of the tunnel and looked around. Army guys were lying in their bunks along the tunnel wall. The Army was there, and we were the ones standing in columns of fours about to engage invaders in the middle of the night.

I was within ten feet of this one group of bunks attached to the tunnel wall. This one guy was staring at us, so I said, "Hey!"

"Yeah!" He didn't look too interested in our assembly.

"You guys'd better get your rifles and get with it here. The damn Japs are landing out here on the end of the island. In fact, why don't you come on and go with us?"

"We won't," he said. "We can't do that."

"Whaddaya mean, you can't do that?" We were flabbergasted.

"We're noncombatants," he said, shifting slightly on his bunk.

I say, "Whaddya mean, noncombatants?"

"We're Quartermaster Corps. Noncombatants."

"Do you think the *Japs* are gonna know the difference?" I said.

He shrugged his shoulders.

I said, "*God damn*! I'm a yeoman in the Navy. I'm not supposed to be here either, but the Japs are coming. You'd better get a gun."

They did not move. They stayed in there in their bunks. Well, that immediately soured me on noncombatants. The only noncombatants I knew of in the Navy were the chaplains, and I think even they carried guns for self-protection.

I was armed with a .45 Colt pistol in my leather hip holster, a single ammo bandolier where only half the pouches contained thirty-ought-six shells for a World War I bolt-action Springfield rifle I had never seen before. At best, I could hope to get off one shot before dropping on my knee to reload and re-aim. In basic training we had been taught about shipboard fighting, but nothing about ground-warfare tactics. Our last live firing had been in basic training or at one of the firing ranges in mainland China. For most of us, that was a couple of years ago. Let me see. Can we remember to take the safety off after we are to engage the enemy? Things were not looking good here, but our naval squad was equally equipped, trained, and prepared.

We went out into the moonlit night and engaged the enemy. Some of us went around to the Bataan side of the mountain and walked right into the direct line of fire. I caught a piece of shrapnel in my leg. Thank God, it was lodged in the fleshy part of my knee and it was spent. I reached down and jerked the sliver of metal out.

I fired, reloaded, and fired several more times. I am not certain if I hit anybody, and do not know if their advance was turned back or if they held their position. My knee was giving me trouble, so we hightailed it back into Malinta Tunnel. I kept moving until I reached Queens Tunnel, the Navy tunnel. Some of the guys stayed with me while I got my leg patched up. It was not badly hurt, and I had in my favor the healing powers of youth.

For the surrender on May 6, 1942, we were ordered to destroy our weapons before presenting ourselves to the enemy. One guy demolished his rifle by hitting the butt on one of the stumps left by prior Jap bombardment. It was loaded and went off. He shot himself in the thigh and, though wounded, did not die. We were ordered to wait in Malinta Tunnel.

I thought it strange that they did not have enough room for us during the bombardment, but now it was okay to wait in the tunnel for the surrender. It was crowded, though with enough room to sit and snooze. There was no room to lie down except for those who had already been assigned a bunk, so I moved about. I preferred Queens Tunnel, the Navy tunnel, to the Army tunnel, Malinta, so I trudged on over there.

We knew we were in "deep shit with no means of locomotion" as we awaited processing. We discussed surrender with a couple of naval officers awaiting the same fate. One of the officers I recognized from Admiral Hart's command. He and the other officers were schooled in the Geneva Convention rules but had no experience or knowledge of the horrors of the enemy. Thinking that I might not be alive later to tell him this, I told him how much I had enjoyed working under his command. Sensing a finality in my remarks, he said, "Kidd, don't worry about it. This is all taken in stride under the provisions of the Geneva Convention, and we will be treated humanely during our captivity." Humane treatment was the furthest thing from my mind. I had seen what the Japs had done in China. I was under the impression that none of us would even be around in another couple of days anyway.

We had seen the Japs and their treatment of captured Chinese. We had heard horror stories and had read accounts of them in the Manila newspapers. While in China, I had personally seen some running Chinaman shot dead by a group of Jap soldiers. In another city, we had accidentally run across a back-street execution of a coolie—arms tied behind his back, blindfolded, down on his knees, and a pistol shot to the head administered by a Jap officer. We did not know if this was the execution of some deserving criminal or the disposal of a civilian who had fought against an invading enemy. We did not stick around to find out. We knew they were ruthless.

Those who had been in Queens Tunnel the longest preferred the area nearest the entrance. It was cooler—well, make that less hot. With some air circulation it was not as stuffy as the back part of the tunnel, where a lateral passageway opened to the outside. Here in the dark with water and very little food our CINCAF awaited our fate.

I thought of our CINCAF officer's statement the next morning when I awoke. Standing at the doorway of one of the laterals to Queens Tunnel was an angry-looking Jap Marine with a fixed bayonet. He was hollering in Japanese and pointing at us. He and a couple more Jap soldiers issued commands in their language, but by hand motion it was clear to us that he wanted us to exit the tunnel and strip down completely. We were ordered to put our shoes in one pile, socks in another, and to make separate piles for shirts, shorts, and trousers. Then they lined us up in columns of four, on this narrow mountain road.

The Jap Marine took his rifle with fixed bayonet and approached us. Where the Americans had their dog tags around their neck, he stuck the bayonet up underneath the chain and tugged it tight. *Wu-ch-i-i-ik!* Just like that, the bayonet cut off each of the dog tags.

When he began yelling again, the first group was already totally naked and in formation. I was in the second group, naked too, but not quite in formation. Others behind us were still in the process of shedding their clothes.

I was not surprised. I was scared, but not surprised. I thought the end would come and there was not a damn thing we could do about it.

Though none of us spoke Japanese, it was clear from his motions and waving what he was ordering us to do. Quick jabbing motions with his bayonet to the guy on the outside line meant, "You'd better move." We moved slowly from our piles of garments and shoes, which made him more animated and angry. He wanted us to go faster.

He motioned us to go over to the cliff side of the mountain road, where we could see waves from the blue ocean crashing white on the brown rocks two hundred feet below. There, as if by herd instinct, we all halted, nude, gaunt beings, a hundred yards from our stacks of clothing on this shell-pocked road, ten yards from a two-hundred-foot flight to death.

There was no mistake about it. To us reluctant lemmings, his poking rifle gestures meant jump.

The USS *Nevada* pulls away from burning ships. This was the first U.S. Navy ship assignment for John Kidd, who was not aboard her on December 7, 1941, but had taken ships of lesser size and station to see the Orient. (U.S. Navy photo)

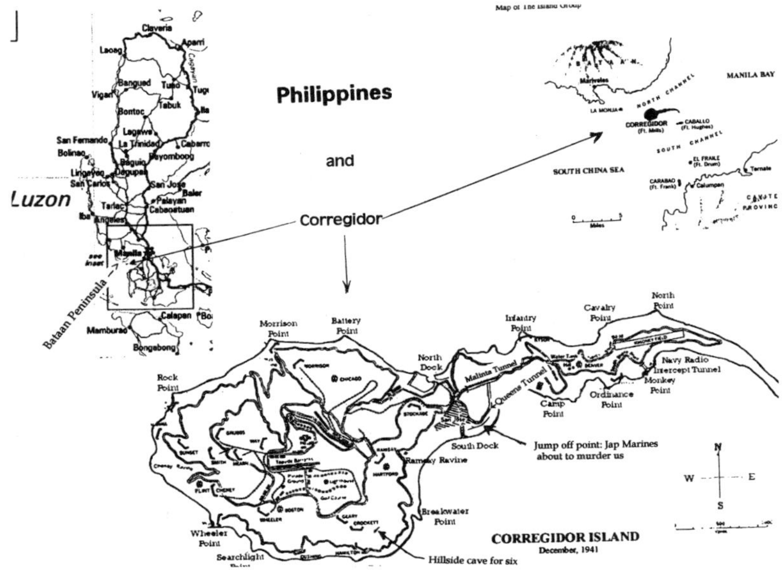

Map of Corregidor. No room for John Kidd at Malinta or Queens Tunnel, so he and others were outside during the bombardment. Location points for his hillside communal fox-hole for six. Location point where Japanese Marines almost murdered 200 Americans who had already surrendered. (U.S. Navy photo)

Three of the four American POWs who were beaten continuously for three days while being given no food or water—for trying to escape. With the entire POW camp made to watch, the four were executed after digging their own graves. (U.S. Navy photo)

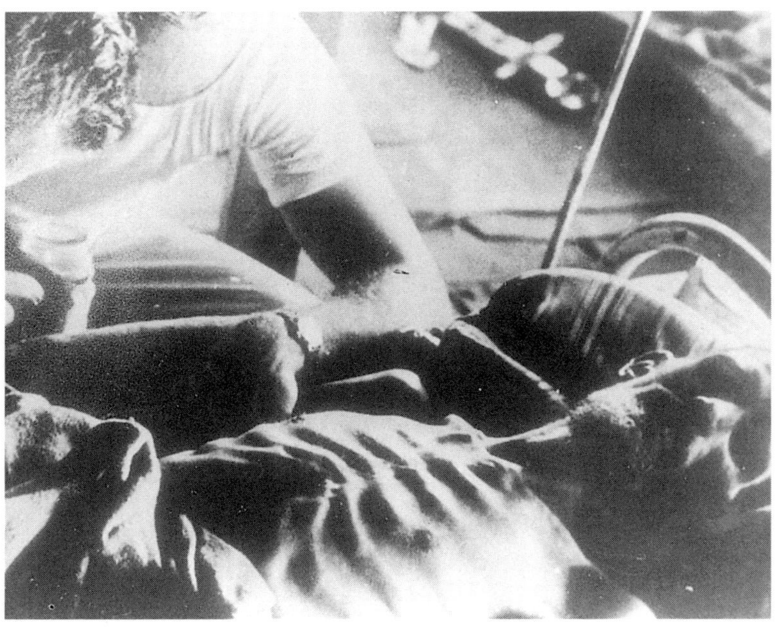

POW showing starvation upon release. This is not a picture of John Kidd, but after his experimental surgery performed by Japanese doctors, with the complications cared for by the British physicians, John Kidd weighed eighty-six pounds and looked like this. (Source: American Ex-POW Association)

Group picture of just-released POWs standing outside.
(Source: American Ex-POW Association)

Group picture of just-liberated hospitalized POWs. (Source: American Ex-POW Association)

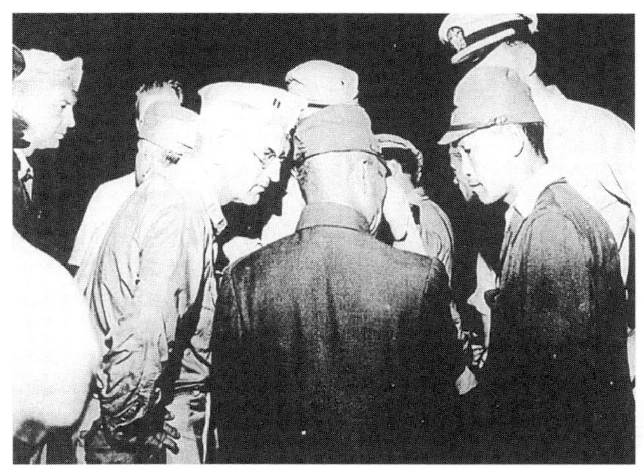

Conference at Aomori Japanese POW camp. This was the next-to-last camp to which John Kidd had been moved before the war ended. (Source: American Ex-POW Association)

U.S. prisoners in the Philippines. John Kidd had endured the "no-shade wait" in the tropical sun early in his captivity. (Source: American Ex-POW Association)

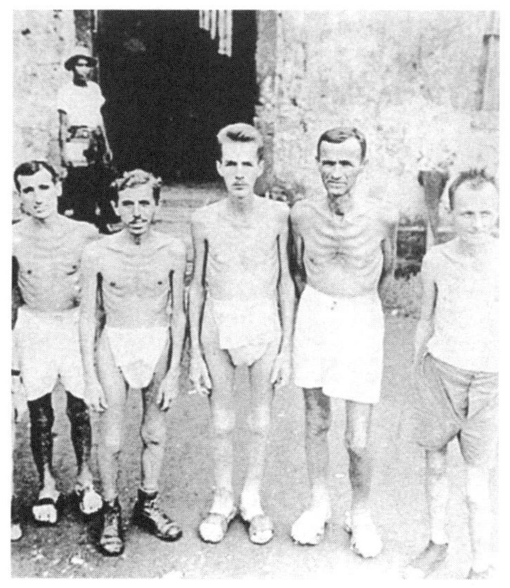

Liberated U.S. prisoners after three years in Bilibad. John Kidd had been in Bilibad early in the war, but had been transported via Hellship to Japan. It illustrates the severe starvation in Japanese POW camps. (Source: American Ex-POW Association)

Gaunt prisoners cheer their liberators while proudly waving the Stars and Stripes. (Source: American Ex-POW Association)

Nine

Guests of the Emperor

I had come a long way for this—unbelievable. I had a long way to go, but two hundred feet below was not the option I wanted, but there it was. Thirty feet away, then two hundred feet down, my trip halfway around the world would end; from Tyler, Texas to Corregidor by way of China; all starting with a short trip from Tyler to Marshall, Texas at the naval recruiting office.

My idyllic summer life of childhood with my grandparents in Tyler contrasted with the workaholic atmosphere my stepfather in Houston had shown me during my late-childhood years. Tired of his constant promoting frugality and long working hours to build character, I ran away from Houston and sought the refuge of the "good life" at my grandparents', but found that jobs in a small town were limited and advancement opportunities few.

After discussing deep subjects of life one day with this native Tyler boy two years my senior, whose name I cannot recall, we concluded that we ought to do something with our lives. We were going nowhere here. Since we couldn't get jobs that paid anything, maybe we ought to join the military. That would solve it. "I'm only fifteen," I said, "Too young."

"Awwww," he said. "Just tell 'em you're seventeen."

That sounded good to me, so we hitchhiked fifty miles over to Marshall, Texas to the Navy recruiting station. When we arrived, it was closed for some holiday. We didn't have any money for a room, so we slept in the stairwell in the county courthouse.

The next morning we went to this restaurant across the street from the courthouse and explained to the owner that we had tried to see the Navy recruiter the day before, but he was gone. We were awful hungry.

The kind man spared us a breakfast.

Afterwards, we went over to the station, where the Navy recruiter gave us some applications and tests. Believe it or not, I passed those tests.

"Go back and we'll call you when a vacancy occurs," said the recruiter. "With the Depression still on, we got enough volunteers for military service, so you'll be put on a waiting list of twelve to eighteen months.

"By the way, how old are you, Kidd?"

"Well," I said, "I'm, uh, seventeen."

"Now?" He looked perplexed. "How 'bout sixteen?"

I said, "Seventeen!"

"Okay," he said. "You need a sworn affidavit from your mother stating you are seventeen years old. She is your legal guardian, and you must have her authority to enlist."

Oh, he knew damn well I wasn't seventeen. I hadn't even started shaving.

In that interminable moment when guttural Japanese through clenched teeth met English-only ears and bodily fears, nothing happened. No one moved in those long lines of nude American men in columns caught between the fixed bayonets of the uniformed Japs who had ordered us to strip down. The Japs made it perfectly clear they wanted each prisoner to cross the mountain road and jump off the two-hundred-foot cliff.

There was no escape. You would have been just as dead from being shot as from jumping. If they wanted us over the cliffs, we would make them work for it. They could toss us over after they had murdered us, so we froze. We would soon die naked on this ugly road stripped of vegetation from months of shelling before. The first outside guy was inches from being stuck by a Jap bayonet.

We heard virulent screaming in Japanese from where the road climbed around the mountain in front of us. It was higher-pitched, more urgent, and authoritative. We thought, *These bastards are going to have some sort of ceremony as they massacre us.* The Jap marines about to kill us yelped back, but in a subservient tone to the one coming from the road.

Two Jap officers had come upon the situation and were yelling at the bayonet toters pushing us to jump. The officers chewed out the marines, who stood at attention and said nothing. It was verbal slapping, but nothing physical. The bayonet toters saluted and immediately retreated down the road.

The officer spoke some English and explained that these were Japanese Marines who had made an earlier landing and were unaware the surrender had taken place. They thought they had captured us. According to their Bushido military tradition, the Jap Marines were punishing "cowards" who wouldn't fight, not bullying surrendered soldiers honoring an order.

The officer who halted our murder told us to get our clothes, get back into the tunnel, and stay there until other orders had been issued. That was all he had to say. In the scramble to get clothes, any clothes, I got a pair of size nine and a half shoes. I wondered about the poor guy that had to wear my size sevens. It was grab the first clothes and shoes you could and run back into the tunnel before they changed their minds.

The Japs marched us from Queens Tunnel back to the U.S. Army Transportation Department on Corregidor, further out on the "tail of the tadpole" almost to Monkey Point, where a number of garages were collectively called "The 92nd Garage." They parked all the prisoners on the twenty acres of pavement in the hundred-degree sun. Luckily, we had brought a little food along with us for our three-day encampment. Some work details were assigned to scrounge around for other food that we were able to cook on bonfires in the prisoners' area. A tattered tent remnant from the bombardment stretched between poles served as an umbrella to shade our group of a dozen men from the relentless sun. Others had similar ragged shades, but not everyone did. It was: Share a little shade, share a little burn.

Work details were drawn from this pool of prisoners for the clean-up of the prior bombardment. All trees had been reduced to fragments of firewood logs and kindling. Decaying bodies covered with black or green flies, American and Jap, were scattered everywhere. Occasionally a monkey had likewise succumbed in the dispute between his higher-evolved cousins. A decision to shape up made in the enemy hierarchy was probably for public health reasons. Cremate the bodies and consume the plentiful firewood scattered about.

Some work details took care of the Americans; others were assigned a Japanese cremation detail. I am not certain how the American dead were handled, but I saw our detail put two more Jap bodies on a big pyre. Like others, I gathered more wood for the burn which added more heat to the already stifling outside temperature.

Our detail worked near a one-room tan canvas tent just outside the Malinta Tunnel entrance. A very important officer in shiny brown boots with a Samurai sword swinging at his side oversaw all the work from his tent and was attended by an orderly. Lesser-ranking Japs were scattered around supervising the Americans.

The water station for thirsty GIs was near the tent. We drank from the spigot of a captured U.S. rubberized canvas bag just like the one outside our communal fox hole last week. I limped from my shrapnel wound and could not match some of my healthier counterparts in tossing wood on the fire. As I approached the water bag I noticed the important officer glancing in my direction. While I stood there alone, he walked up. I thought he almost took pity on me for limping, but I was fearful that he would deem me a "slacker."

At his approach, I saluted, the military courtesy of any lower rank to an officer and a necessity when you are held captive. I held my canteen cup at a respectful stance.

"Good morning," he said in perfect English. Factual.

"Good morning, sir," I replied. I was in shock. English.

"Would you like to come in and sit down?" I followed.

We walked to the shade of his tent, the only one around. I thought maybe this guy is the run-of-the-mill Japanese instead of the crack combat troops we had been up against. Maybe our murder attempt by the Jap marines was the anomaly and this represented the norm. Japanese officers had halted our murder. After all, up to this point, we had not seen any abuse of the captee by the captor on Corregidor. Except for not being fed much, we were not mishandled.

He introduced himself and probably gave me his rank. I was so stunned that I cannot remember either to this day.

I stood before him as he sat on his bunk. I politely declined his offer of hot tea, but we talked. He explained that until recently he had been a college student, somewhere up East in the United States. He went home to visit his parents in Japan and, while he was there, got put into a tight position: Take a commission in the Japanese Army or else.

He was almost apologetic in his approach, and said something to me I found most astounding. He said that he knew the United States was going to win and that "Japan had no ability to produce the necessary equipment to win this war."

I was stupefied and said nothing, fearing that if anyone heard him, they would cut his head off for saying it and mine off for hearing it. I sensed that he was almost contrite. He thanked me for helping to take care of their dead.

We talked of the cremation duty, and I asked him how they were going to distinguish the ashes of their dead from the wood ashes of the cremation. He told me that after the fires had burned down, they had "special people" to do that. I could see no way that anyone could tell the difference between wood ashes and human remains. Ashes these "special people" determined to be the deceased soldier were put into a white-silk-covered box with Japanese writing of the deceased's name. The container, about the size of today's family-size Kleenex box, formed the pendant held by a loose scarf draped around another comrade's neck. It stayed with the chosen fellow soldier for his personal delivery to the deceased's family back in Japan.

Though I doubted that anyone could tell the difference between body and wood ash with the fires so hot, I was in no position to dispute. I thought many times over this encounter, for if it had been overheard and understood by his side, I am certain death would have been the reward for his compassion. I do not know if he survived the war or what happened. After I left his command tent, I never again saw him. I did not know it at the time, but he was the single island of an honorable Japanese I would meet in an ocean of Japs in the next three years.

I had mixed feelings that night about my captivity. Maybe the American officers I had talked to were right. Maybe our captors would honor the Geneva Convention.

Maybe what we had seen in China was aberrant gangsterism. I did not speak of this incident to my fellow prisoners lest, in its telling and retelling, the story might change, like in the childhood game of "gossip." They might construe that I had a tea party with the enemy, rather than part of a short conversation between two humans whose countries were at war with one another. Except for the stripping and murder attempt by the Jap marines, my captivity had been relatively decent up to now. You expected to be on a work detail. A little more food would have been appreciated, but we had not eaten well when we were under American control anyway.

One morning they searched every one of us. These guards made us empty our pockets, and they greedily transferred our wallets, rings, money, and watches into their own pockets. At this point we realized that we were not dealing with a Geneva Convention–aware enemy. These Bushido-proud Japanese military men were nothing more than a bunch of thieves and *gangu*—gangsters in their language—who had now lost face. They herded us into a cargo ship bound for Manila.

"Standing room only" was the condition two stories below an open hatch accessible by a rope ladder. We made the two-hour trip across Manila Bay. It gets hot in the hold, and thoughts of "I'm glad this is a short trip" flashed through my mind. Instead of going into the dock for mooring, they steered the bow onto a sandy beach and yelled, "Jump off!"

We jumped from both sides into water about six feet deep, but a lot of short fellows, especially those who could not swim, floundered and would have drowned had it not been for taller people helping. Stumbling ashore, we were met by a platoon of armed guards, a shiny phalanx of fixed bayonets indicating that we should form four dripping columns for their "victory parade" down the civilian thoroughfares to Bilibad Prison. Mean and menacing in their fresh uniforms, these Japs were an extension of the last ones on Corregidor who had stolen everything from us except the clothes on our backs. Maybe the rags had been too tattered to steal. Maybe the new guard detail was mad because the old one had already stolen everything valuable.

They slapped us with rifle butts for any real or imagined infractions in rules known only to them. They glared at us, daring us to attempt escape so they might brutally display the prowess of the Rising Sun. They were itching for a fight, so we dared not look in their direction or make any move or gesture they might interpret as our disliking the hostility they showed us. It became brutally clear: no Geneva rules here. Bow or be beaten?

We marched by the apartments, hotel, and restaurant where I had been bivouacked before the war. Out of the corner of my eye, I saw my girlfriend standing out on the curb watching us go by. "Momma, there's John," she hollered. Of course I didn't dare say anything or even look in her direction because you might get bayonetted or shot if you did. Worse yet, she or her mother might get bayonetted or shot—after being raped first. Consequently, I just kept on going. I never saw the two women again.

They marched us to Bilibad Prison, an antiquated facility that had been utilized by the constabulary before the Spanish-American War. In this century-old prison they served us some watery rice soup with a bit of lamb and a piece of fat floating on top. It was the best soup I had ever eaten; but I've never had lamb since.

The next day they loaded us into boxcars that were smaller than those in the States, more like the European boxcars made for narrow-gauge tracks. They crowded us into these boxcars in the same fashion that Nazis would load the Jews half the world away, though we would not know this until after the war had ended. As it was in the ship cargo hold, standing room only was the order of the day as they slammed the doors shut. In the stifling heat, there were no latrine/head facilities, so the corner walls became the rolling dumping ground.

We disembarked at some little town, and they marched us about twenty miles into the jungle and up the mountains to our first prison camp, called Cabanatuan #3. The men who were ill and in pretty bad shape from the trip did poorly on the force-march in the hundred-degree temperature. One chief died of a heart attack outside the camp upon our arrival.

We had no knowledge of the infamous Bataan Death March that had taken place a month before ours, hearing about it later as some POW transferees from Camp O'Donnell came in. Our march was brutal, but it seemed as though the Jap captors really wanted us to make it to Cabanatuan #3. It is obvious that the infamous sixty-five-mile Bataan Death March through the steamy jungle forced men who had had nothing to eat or drink to die all along the way. More than 7,000 prisoners died on the Bataan Death March, one-third American, two-thirds Filipino. This was a massacre in march time so that Camp O'Donnell would have no prisoners.

The world's most infamous march under Jap direction was an example of how bad is bad, how evil is evil, an event whose effect easily ranks with the Holocaust for hatred. Unfortunately, its historical existence has been relegated from a "never again" stance to one of "Let's don't teach it in history; the gentle Japanese of today could never have been naughty like that."

Our Jap guards were regular army, veterans that had been in campaigns, like China. They set up their guardhouse, and we had to salute it each time we passed by. It was very odd. If one of them walked up to us, we had to salute, or get our face smashed with a rifle butt. Any type of military salute was demanded of you, American, British, or Japanese. Anything, but you had to snap to it quickly and make it look honorable. The salute was demanded, though they preferred the "polite" bow known in their culture and displayed by them to their officers. Salute or be slapped: your choice. Sometimes they slapped us for reasons known only to them; the only common denominator being that the person being hit possessed white skin and round eyes. They had strict rules.

The food consisted of a sweet potato vine boiled in water as a soup—not the potato, just the vine. They added rice sweepings off of the floor of the various warehouses that contained little brown-headed rice worms. It gave a real definition to the term "dirty rice," a term not widely used in American culture then. They cooked worms and all, and gave us about half a canteen cup of rice and a half canteen cup of that potato vine soup twice a day.

I was fortunate to have my own canteen cup, though I do not know what happened to my canteen. Lost, or stolen, it was not with me. Other prisoners fashioned their own cup out of used tin cans, a little tricky when the original opener had been a hand-held one leaving the edges looking like they had been trimmed with pinking shears.

We stayed there through July; then August dragged on into September. Nearly everyone there developed pellagra. I did. My tongue swelled up and split open. All cracks bled, were infected, and hurt like hell. With thick tongues, we all mumbled like you would with a full mouth. My shrapnel wound had partially healed by then, but I developed an infection on my right foot. It was swollen, and the skin between my big toe and the next was cracking open. This wound was leaking pus and hurt constantly.

It cured itself; only God knows how. I washed it, but I had nothing to put on it to help. No iodine, mercurochrome, alcohol, hydrogen peroxide, or any of the things in common use prior to the antibiotic era. If they marched you anywhere and you dropped behind, you got bayonetted or even shot. Bayonetting seemed to be preferred. So I walked on my heels to stay alive. It was dry season and dust was everywhere.

In the hundred-plus temperature and high humidity I wore a long-sleeve shirt at all times, ostensibly to keep from being sunburned, but really to hide my tattoos. In American naval culture, tattoos were a rite of passage and a proud personal display of ship and country. In Japanese culture, tattoos were worn by gangsters, *gangu,* the really tough people. I did not wish to have a test of toughness inflicted on me when the tester had total power and a rifle butt—and the tested, the role of being beaten without protesting. Our last "bath" was when the Japs dumped us in the saltwater shallows of Manila Bay back in May. Though my shirt stank and could practically stand in the corner all by itself, I kept it on. All of us who "bathed" together four months ago smelled the same.

In the Japanese Army, the disciplinary procedure was simple. Officers would line up their own troops and slap the fools who broke the rules. The slap of the offender in the face with bare hands and public humiliation was considered to be "corrective discipline."

Higher rank slapped lower rank. Lower rank slapped the lowest, who had nobody to slap—that is, until we came along. The lower the rank of the Jap guard, the harsher the slapper hit the slappee. So it was nothing out of the ordinary for a Jap guard to call you to attention and then haul off and slap you. There was absolutely nothing you could do about it. If you even looked like you objected, you got beaten until you were unconscious.

Four of our guys escaped, wounding the Japanese *Bushida* pride. They were captured and returned to the camp. Each was tied to a single wooden railroad tie, hands bound behind his back to his heels in a kneeling position. The Japs crammed a wooden four-by-four between their thighs and the back of their knees so they could not sit down. It forced them to kneel forward with the weight of their body on their knees. Every time a Jap would walk by, he would slap our man, the Jap's rifle butt being preferred to his hand.

For three days, the Japs hit and kicked them any way they could. The men were given no food or water, and were about to pass out in misery. Fellow prisoners were allowed on two occasions to give them some water, not an example of Japanese mercy, but to keep them alive for another Jap slap.

On the afternoon of the third day, the Japs cut the four-by-four posts from their legs. Unable to walk, they were dragged out behind the barracks. The Japs called everyone out to witness these sick and weary men being made to dig their own graves. When the graves got knee deep, they stood our men in one end. A firing squad of low ranks executed them. After they fell face first in their shallow graves, a Jap officer walked around and shot each one in the back of his head. The prisoners were ordered to cover each executed man with loose dirt.

Then they divided each group of prisoners into squads of ten men. We were warned to check on the others. If one man out of those ten escaped, the other nine would be shot—the prisoners were responsible to stop other escapes.

There were no more attempted breaks while I was there, but I was not there much longer. Although the Japs had work details for us that went outside the prison compound, I was too sick and wounded for them to put me on one. The Japs got the word to us that they were going to ship some of prisoners to Japan. From Cabanatuan #3, I was in the first group shipped.

We had to march back down to the railhead, and get in the boxcars to travel back to Manila, standing all the way. We stayed in Bilibad Prison overnight. From there we went to Pier 7 to a waiting Jap ship.

The outside temperature was high in the double digits to low in the triple on this typical tropical September day. We were marched up the gangway like a herd of cattle. Hurry. Hurry. I do not know the name of our ship, and did not really care. The something *Maru*. All Jap ships are named something Maru. I did not want to get poked with a bayonet. My foot condition had improved. I could rest my overworked heels and put some weight on my less-troubled toes.

Sixty-three years later I would learn this ship was named the *Toko Maru*, and that it was the fifth of September, 1942 that we departed with 500 prisoners crammed in the hold. In this moment I wanted to avoid provoking guards whose verbal language I did not understand, and whose body language spewed contempt.

The ship holds are normally used to carry cargo. Our ship had two forward and one aft, with midships for the bridge and engine room. Each hold had a sturdy metal wall standing two-and-a-half feet above deck boards guarding the twelve by thirty-foot opening. Its boom normally lowered wooden crates of general wares or cargo nets of hundred-kilogram rice bags to the bulk storage area below. For us, rope ladders had been thrown over the side and dangled two stories down to the hold floor. The human cargo had to step lively or get bayonetted.

I was among the first dozen to climb down. I found that the hold had been modified to carry people, short people. Its port-to-starboard width was fifty feet, and its length was eighty feet. As I descended, I saw four decks in the hold arranged like big shelves around the space of the hatch. The Japs had modified the twenty-foot height by adding I-beam steel half way down. This was a sturdy support for its own center wood deck plus two more wooden decks, one five feet above center and the other five feet below. Thus with some of the space taken for the boards themselves, there was four and a half feet of usable height. While this may have been a little cozy for the Japan out-bound cargo of fresh Nip troops, it forced us taller Occidentals, the Japan in-bound cargo, to stand in an awkward stooped position, backs semi-bent forward.

Though I was glad to leave the blazing sun behind, I soon realized it was dark below, the opening being the only connection to the outside world. At the bottom of the ladder, we had to disburse into the sealed-off area of this ship that had no facilities for relieving your daily toilet functions. To the deck temperature, add another twenty degrees for the inside of the steel cargo holds; then make the humidity 98 percent. The Japs crammed us shoulder to shoulder in those ships, with no room to sit down. To lie down was out of the question. Shoulder to shoulder, face to face, we smelled each other, all contributing to the common stink.

The farther from the sunlight streaming in the open hatch, the darker your space was. Then the Japs slid a steel inverted "T"-bar into the notches at the bow and stern ends of the hatch walls. It served like the tie beam of a house for many notched two-by-twelve boards to form a "roof." Now all were in the dark. Now all had even less air to circulate or breathe.

The bottom deck was designated for head usage. The Japs lowered two five-gallon buckets to relieve yourself in, which made for lines to get to the bottom deck. Lucky us; we were already there. Less standing in line, but the smell more than made up for the shorter line. Soon everyone had diarrhea, and spontaneous "relief" came on the way to the Jap bucket. In a matter of days, the rest of the decks smelled as bad as the bottom. I had diarrhea and pellagra, and now the beginning of beriberi. We did not know it was beriberi, but we knew the symptoms everybody had, abdominal and leg swelling with a burning sensation in our legs. The reduced rations while we were fighting the delaying action in Bataan and being bombarded on Corregidor, coupled with the poor nutrition after capture, were having an unhealthy effect. As we continued, the stench of four bath-free months in the tropics became less of a problem. We could no longer smell each other because the stench of urine and feces was overpowering.

There was overpowering thirst brought on by the heat and humidity. Some had hallucinations. It was truly survival of the fittest. Crowded conditions led to intolerance of fellow internees and fights among ourselves, usually about the time to go to sleep. The "fights" were more verbal, and there were threats like "Get off my feet" and "Don't lean on me." We were all too weak to either defend ourselves or carry on aggression against another beyond a shoving match. Only when a guy collapsed and we could no longer hold him up we did move over, squeeze against each other harder, and make room for him to fall.

History would later record our transportation correctly as being in "Hell Ships." These unmarked Japanese freighters were used to transport POWs during WWII to Japan for slave duty. Allied forces, who had no way of knowing POWs were in the cargo holds, frequently torpedoed or attacked them from the air, sometimes sinking the hapless cargo. Thousands perished during the war. The worst sinking was the *Arisan Maru,* torpedoed by an American submarine on October 24, 1944 with 1795 of the 1800 POWs aboard perishing in the South China Sea. None of us aboard our Hellship knew this at the time.

We steamed out of Manila Bay, with a destination of Japan by way of Formosa. The Jap guards did lower down some five-gallon buckets of drinking water after we got under way, but it was not nearly enough. Everybody was thirsty. The Japs quit pulling up the loaded latrines and heaped-full heads, their five-gallon cans for our personal relief. We had to use one part of the hold, but it all sloshed as a unit of filth.

A lot of guys ran amuck and died. Some of them lost their mind totally, drinking their own urine or the blood from the open wounds of other prisoners. I did not see either, but I heard stories. I knew that drinking your own sweat might have the same effect as drinking sea water. It only made you more thirsty. The heat and stench were horrible. Imagine standing wall-to-wall with other people in a sauna where there are four inches of sewage backup and half the people have soiled their trousers.

You couldn't get on the five-gallon cans in time, and in getting there you had a line. By that time your diarrhea cramp had taken its toll. Your trousers were soiled again. Most would defecate in their pants. If you didn't, the next guy had. You were pressed against him, breathing his air, so why not feel and smell his shit. He was smelling and feeling yours anyway. That heat. It was unbelievable. Hellship!

These ships were not marked in any way whatsoever as being POW ships, as called for by the Geneva Convention. One could not distinguish them from the usual cargo, supply or troop ships of the Rising Sun. The stench in the hold was so bad that even the Japs decided the limited latrine facilities below were not sufficient. Thus it was that they built an "open head" long enough for six men to use at a time over the side of the ship. This platform extended from boards anchoring it to the deck. It had a wall sea-side but no roof. We had direct access to a place on the two two-by-twelve boards braced eighteen inches apart. You straddled or squatted on them over the open slit between as the ship rolled and pitched with the waves. You aimed to the water twenty-five feet below, and your business fell directly into the ocean.

One day I happened to be topside when all of a sudden I heard this really excited jabbering. Of course, I did not understand Japanese, but the ship started turning sharply. I looked up and this sailor was pointing out to the ocean. There were these two fishlike streaks trailing white in the blue coming toward us. The captain turned the ship toward them. *Scheewwww,* right along our sides those torpedoes went. We were between them. They missed. I'll tell you what. I was ready to visit that "open head" again.

I had no desire to go back down into the hold, but there was little choice when guards urged with bayonets.

Back in the hold I stepped off the twisting rope ladder and told those guys, "Man, they just made a torpedo run on us."

"Who in the hell did that?" they asked.

"Who the hell do you think? American torpedoes went by."

"How do you know that?"

"Well, who else's got submarines out here?"

"Oh. Okay."

The rest of the trip was uneventful, and we arrived in Formosa five hours later. Our topside view from the toilet showed us anchored in the harbor, not at a dock. It took a long time for them to assemble a convoy. Our stinking ship hold was not hosed; nor were we given opportunity to take a bath. The trip out of the stinking hold to have a bowel movement on the outrigger head was the high point of the day. As our fellow prisoners began to die off, we got a little more space. The guys would take turns sitting down and getting up. It helped a little bit just to be able to sit down and sleep in shifts. I have no idea what happened to the guys that died on that trip. Perhaps they were just buried at sea. At least the Japs got them out of the hold of the ship where we were.

They finally assembled a convoy with destroyer escorts, and we headed for Japan. Those who stood nearest the bulkhead and leaned against the ship noted that the searing-hot steel became warm, and then cool, and then cold. Our topside-toilet view was no longer rolling ocean, but Tokyo Bay. As soon as they pulled us from our sardine-can stance, freezing November weather trampled us through soiled and tattered tropical garments.

My later acquaintance Carruthers was somewhere on this ship, too. He was interned at a prison camp in the immediate Tokyo area while I was put in another group. It was almost Thanksgiving of 1942, and we were freezing to death in Japan. Our tropical shorts meant nothing, and those few who had blankets snuggled in them tightly to keep from freezing to death. Those without blankets just stood there and shook.

They selected a group of about four hundred for transportation by electric train to Kobe, Japan, not standing in boxcars or cattle cars, but sitting in regular passenger cars. Amazing. None of us had bathed in six months. Our shaded brown and tan summer uniforms were flaking, but not all brown was bits of thread. Caked diarrhea stains, dry and flaky, mixed with body lice were inadvertent "gifts" from prisoners to the Emperor's loyal subjects who would later sit in the car. Civilians rode with us, but not in the same car. For the moment, we were out of the miserable cold. We were thankful. Happy Thanksgiving.

The next afternoon we arrived at a prison camp called *Yodogawa Bunsho.* We got off the train, and they lined us up outside this big steel mill. We stood at attention out there in the cold. An important-looking Jap with a cheese knife and his less important civilian interpreter got up on a speaker stand. "Cheese knife" was our slang term for the Samurai sword the high-ranking Japanese carried. When raised high over their heads with the blade pointed to the enemy, tradition said it brought out the ancient collective spirit to fight in battle. Today, against rifles and machine guns, it was useless—good only to cut cheese with. In our mind's eyes, and under these circumstances, we imagined a "cheese knife" being carried by a big rat—a big Jap rat; but we had to remember that these rats were in control. Don't dare let the one who is carrying the "cheese knife" know your thoughts. You will be made dead. Pay attention, now. The interpreter is about to tell us what the rodent jabber means.

"Welcome to Japan," the interpreter told us. We silently gasped at "welcome," but he was dead serious.

"You should be thankful that you are guests of the Emperor instead of dead," he continued. We collectively thought: *Guests? Guests of the Emperor? Is there something missing in the translation.*

"To show your gratitude to the Emperor for his mercies, you should work very hard, because you are his guests. You should reward him by your toils on any work details assigned."

One of the first duties of a "guest of the Emperor" was to say your assigned prison number. To do this, you had to be able to count in Japanese, which none of us could speak. To insure you did this correctly, the Japs provided us with teachers. After the roll call, *tenko,* you were to count off, *bongo.* An interpreter worked with a prison guard and numbers were assigned. You learned to count off in Japanese: *Ichi, Ni, San, Shi, Go;* for 1, 2, 3, 4, 5; *Roku, Shichi, Hachi,* 6, 7, 8; *Ku, Ju* for 9, 10. The Japanese "I" sounds like the English "e." They were very patient with our learning the first two times around, supplementing the third go-round and beyond with a five-foot bamboo stick, two inches in diameter, modified at one end by splitting the bamboo into small bristles. When they bashed your head or back with this rod, the bamboo bristles spread out for less than a second. When the bristles returned to their former shape, they pinched your hair or skin in between. They snapped the rod back, snatching the pinched skin and appendages and leaving bloody streaks. It did not take long to learn to count in Japanese—at least to know your number.

We were put into the barracks outside Kobe, and by then my legs had begun to swell. The beriberi added itself to the pellagra of many of us, and the diarrhea was going strong in everybody. We all had colds and maybe even pneumonia. We did not know how sick we were, and there was no doctor to tell us. The Japs merely fed us (very little) and divided us into work details.

Inside the barracks, "beds" were a tier of three wooden shelves six feet deep running the length of the building for us to sleep without mattresses. The lowest tier was a foot off the floor, and each shelf was five and a half feet above the lower one. The person on the top level could touch the warehouse ceiling.

When we got to observing that steel mill, we knew beyond a shadow of a doubt that there was no way the Japs could win the war with their antiquated technology of building armaments by hand, by die casting all in sand. By the time they could replenish their losses, American forces, with new equipment, would swamp them.

They poured whatever they were making into a sand mold, then knocked the mold apart to remove the piece and polish it. Even the most unsophisticated of us realized the Japs could not get any appreciable production, especially after we learned how to foul up the diecasts.

We all had long, unclipped fingernails. A nail scratch in the sand of the inside of the mold generated an unwanted little extrusion in the metal of the part being molded. The metal hang meant that the part would not fit when needed. To be caught doing this meant instant death, so it was done only on each third or fourth day.

About the fifth week I got very sick and couldn't go out on the work detail. A lot of guys were sick. A fifth of our camp died or transferred to a hospital camp to die in the first six months we were there. Of the four hundred "guests" who started out from the Philippines together, sixty-eight were dead of starvation, the cold, the beatings, or some combination of the three.

Because I was among the sickest of the prisoners, I was told to stay in the barracks and lie down. When you could not work, they cut your rations in half. To them, it was inefficient to waste food on the nonworking man.

The working "guest of the Emperor" got a small bowl of rice in the morning with a ladle of soup. This soup was mostly water and was made by boiling daikons in water—a lot of water. Daikons, a root food, are two and a half feet long by seven inches in diameter, and taste like radishes.

I continued to deteriorate, and they sent me to their "sick bay." Like the barracks, there was no heat, and the temperature was freezing most days. They kindly put half a cup of canteen water near your head at the bunk. It was so cold that you had to break through the film of ice on top to drink.

The Japs gave each of us a single thin blanket. One guy on wooden slats with one blanket on top was not enough to stay warm, so the guys would double up and that would give us two blankets up on top, wood slats below, and a body thickness of someone else to ward off cold on one side.

I bunked there with a sergeant in the Marines named Andy Anderson from Pampa, Texas. He was so swollen from the beriberi that I have no idea what his normal physical features may have been. My bunking with a fellow Texan was a Jap assignment, a twist of fate rather than a "choose your buddy." It was a fortuitous choice, for the Japs assumed we were both in the pre-death phase of our lives. One might think our conversations would have been philosophical and religious, extended and personal, but they were not.

All we talked about all day long was how to fix food. Never once did we ever discuss sex, girls, or anything like that. The ever-present hunger made you think less about the cold and the physical abuse. Simple bread: toast—one side or both, buttered or not, French toast, how to cook it. Bread to make sandwiches. Get a loaf of bread, unsliced, eat the center out of it and fill it crust to crust with meat or something good to eat. Bread fresh out of the oven. Bread. Bread. Bread. The conversation about food was an escape from all the camp misery. Many times, we spent the whole day talking of all the different ways you could fix just a plain loaf of bread. This simple subject would last from the time we woke up until the time we went to sleep.

Andy was over six feet tall. He was originally stationed in Shanghai to protect American interests but had been evacuated out of Shanghai when it really got to be "sticky wicket" between the Japanese and the British. He was on his way home with a stop in Manila when the war broke out. Since we both hailed from Texas, we had a lot in common.

Andy was sick as I was: swollen legs with pain, protruding abdomen, red, cracked tongue, difficulty in breathing, shivering with cold, and overwhelmed with hunger. We went to sleep one night, and when I woke up the next morning, Andy seemed unusually still and resting quietly. I said something to him; but he did not answer me. I poked him with my elbow. No movement. He was dead. He was lying right beside me, touching me. He died right there beside me.

They removed him from the prisoners' sleep shelves, and the Japs brought in a casket. It was nothing like what you think of as casket-shaped in the United States. This was out of pine boards in the shape of a narrow oblong box, more or less the standard-size for the smaller Japanese deceased. Andy was over six feet tall, the archetypical Texan.

They took his body over there to this box. The Japs could not get the lid closed because his bent knees poked out about nine inches above the edge. The Japs just left him lying askew in the box right across from where we had bunked. In the couple of days his corpse was there, you could hear rats gnawing at night, and see them running in and out of the box during the day.

A couple of days later a Jap death detail returned and broke his legs. They bent his legs backwards over his kneecaps and put the lid on the box. They did all this with me lying there, having to watch them.

They took the box through the door and out of my sight. That was the last I ever saw of Andy Anderson.

Ten
Buttons

All I knew about Andy Anderson was that he was from Pampa, Texas. My best friend had died in a POW camp and been unceremoniously disposed of. I attempted to call the Andersons up at Pampa when I first came back, but I couldn't get through to anybody that knew anything about an Andy Anderson. I don't know who his next of kin was or if he had a next of kin. I am sure he did. Somewhere there was family, somewhere someone loved him, but that somewhere was definitely not Japan.

Maybe love didn't exist on this island at all, or if it did, something got lost in the translation. Maybe I had learned survival skills at home, backgrounded in love I did not understand from my stepfather—not recognized as an unwitting gift to an unwilling youth. My stepfather was a very strict disciplinarian; he punished me as his father had punished him, brutally. In this day and time in our current justice system, I am sure he would have been put in jail. When I look back on it, however, I believe that the discipline he administered enabled me to withstand some of the abuse and hardships I later experienced. It would have been much easier to have given up and died in Japan, but I was stubborn. I knew that if only one POW was to return to the U.S., it was going to be me. I gave no idle thought to giving up. When POWs lying alongside of me said, "I give up," they died within twenty-four hours. I believe my determination to live came from my early childhood in Houston.

In my single-digit and pre-teen years my stepfather took me fishing a couple of times, but he resented taking time off. He accumulated his fortune by being a workaholic, going to the office sometimes at five o'clock in the morning to complete patient bridge and crown work, things done by reliable dental labs today. Not so then. As a perfectionist, he demanded only the best for his patients. His morning office started by eight o'clock, and most of the time he worked to nine P.M. This left him little recreation time other than playing golf on the weekends, and fishing occasionally.

He felt that his workaholic ethic and success patterns should be adopted by me as a child preparing for adulthood. He looked for a cookie-cutter image of himself in me. His demanding guidance became oppressive, leading to a cycle of resistance that commanded more and stronger guidance. He demanded discipleship.

I had the opportunity and money to have done anything I wanted. I could have gone to college to be a physician, dentist, or whatever I chose. Though he had money, he felt that imbuing me with his frugality was prime. He hated paying interest on anything. Though his twenty-year house note at three per cent APR was little monthly cash outlay, he paid it off in three years. I had to buy my own clothes and save for the future out of money from my *two* paper routes and his allowance-for-work program.

I was very unhappy with the austerity, and I thought his stern treatment of me was unreasonable. In fact, when I came back from overseas, he apologized for these things he had done during my youth. I thought it took a pretty big man to do that, for he extended it to my sister. I was very fond of him. I considered him as a dad because I had been with him all my life. Just because I didn't think exactly like he did didn't mean I didn't care for him.

Houston's Southampton was a neighborhood of successful businessmen and professionals. Children do not necessarily appreciate what their fathers do for a living, for they are spending their time at play with other kids.

Bernard DeGeorge's father owned the DeGeroge Hotel downtown and was living with his cousins, Lena and Fred Cannata, our next-door neighbors. Fred Cannata was the manager of the Horwitz Theaters in Houston, the Uptown, Texan, Iris, and Ritz movie houses.

A nephew of Fred and Lena's was Jack Valenti, who showed an unusual and lasting interest in the movie business. He was rarely there as a regular playmate, but I have a picture of us wrestling in the front yard when we were in our sub-teens.

My day began at four A.M. with deliveries of the *Houston Post*, the city's only morning newspaper, before my first class at Sidney Lanier Jr. High School started. We walked a mile and a half each way to and from school, eschewing a city bus because their routes required you to take one to town, get a transfer, then catch another one to your destination, like going from one spoke of a wheel to another by going down to the axle first. Walking took less time. Besides, we didn't spend our money on bus rides. Later, I rode my bike with its wood frame and canvas newspaper racks bolted on the metal luggage rack over the rear wheel, instantly ready for my second after-school paper route, the *Houston Chronicle*. Newspaper home delivery cost ninety cents per month in the 1936–37 era, morning or afternoon.

My home chores included yard work, and once a week I washed my stepfather's new grey Studebaker. Its modern "free wheeling" drive saved gasoline by automatically shifting to neutral when you took your foot off the accelerator.

On the weekends I was his caddy at the BraeBurn Country Club, and sometimes the Houston Country Club off Wayside Drive across town. He paid me fifty cents for caddying eighteen holes. Frugal stepfather. The going rate was eighty cents.

District managers of the *Houston Chronicle* delivered bundles of fifty newspapers each via a panel-stake truck in the afternoon to special spots in town, usually a street corner. Ours was a storefront with an awning so that we could be out of any rain. Carrier boys folded the papers in thirds, tucked them away in their bicycle racks, and tossed them on the home front porch.

My *Houston Chronicle* corner was at the Madison Drug Store on Bissonnett, where my friend Arthur Downey was the soda jerk. Arthur was blind in one eye and classified 4F during World War II. Arthur knew of my plight and heavy punishment. When the situation with my stepfather became unbearable, he invited me to stay with him and his mother.

In a day when schools graduated at grade eleven, I had completed the eighth grade and had fortuitously taken typing along with the usual subjects. The decision to leave home shook me badly, but it ended an intolerable situation. After three weeks with Arthur and his mother, I left for my grandparents in Tyler.

Meanwhile, my own condition deteriorated more.

"He's gonna die," they said, so they loaded me up for transportation from Yodogawa Bunsho Prison Camp on the outskirts of Osaka to the place called Ichioka, where I was supposed to die. On a cool day in the end of April they placed me in the empty bed of a dump truck and hauled my carcass down there like so much garbage.

If one visualizes a football stadium where the back of the bleachers is open, you have half the physical structure of Ichioka Stadium Hospital, located one block off Main Street. The Japs had boarded up the back of an abandoned stadium, forming an opposite wall to the stair-step cement bleachers, giving a roof and one wall. A wooden floor twelve inches off the ground held boarded shelves. In rows of sleeping bays for ten, they tossed one unwashed horse blanket contaminated with fleas, lice, and bedbugs for each prisoner to sleep under.

A straddle-trench latrine twenty feet from the kitchen serviced these needs. Bathing was adjoining the kitchen in one large bathtub eight feet long, five feet wide, and four feet deep constructed of wood. Proximity of food and waste coupled with a scarcity of the former and a plethora of the latter gave an overpowering aroma of bowel and bladder. Disposal of waste was unheard of.

It was first occupied by American prisoners from Guam. Our group had approximately forty-eight Americans: thirty-two army, three navy, five marines, and eight civilians. Coupled with seventy British, twenty Dutch, ten Australians, and the other nationalities, there were a total of 158 POWs. With no medical equipment or medicines, and only one imprisoned English surgeon to make do with nothing, his excellence in care was severely limited. His requests to the Japanese doctors for proper equipment and anethesia to perform amputations or resuturing of previously made Japanese incisions, were answered with, "Let them die." Dr. C.E. Jackson, Lt. Surgeon, Royal British Navy Reserve, was beaten unmercifully for requesting food and medical supplies.

It was a place to await death, but "hospice" is too charitable a term. "Dumping ground" is more descriptive. Since we were unable to work and destined to die, they further reduced our starvation rations. A skimpy half bowl of rice in the morning preceded our noon meal of one ersatz hot dog bun the diameter of a quarter and five inches long. At night, we got half a bowl of rice and some very watery soup that might have a daikon or some green vegetable. Fortunate you were if chance handed you a vegetable in the broth.

Poor provisions predominated. We were allotted approximately 320 grams of rice, barley, vegetables, and bread combined for three meals each day by the prison board in Tokyo for sick prisoners of war. Upon issuing of rations by our Japanese quartermaster, we received approximately 200 grams. Evidently he was buying a home. It was a known fact by the POWs that our Japanese quartermaster and staff were operating one of the largest black markets in Japan. When questioned by the English officer in charge about the shortage of rations, all hands were immediately lined up and beaten with clubs, shoes, and belts by the Japanese officials for daring to question Japanese honesty. Beatings for no reason or according to the whims of the Japs were common. For myself, morale was poor. A British enlisted naval man held religious services once a week. Clothing was not issued. What apparel the men had were tatters salvaged from the dead on the "hellship" transport to Japan, all worn rags.

By that time, my abdomen and my legs had swollen to the point that I could not sit down without holding on to something. I could not bend my legs because they were swollen so badly from beriberi. Beriberi is a disease due to the deficiency of thiamine, or vitamin B-1, in the diet that shows itself with swelling and pain of the lower abdomen and legs. The swelling is due to collection of fluid in the tissues, called edema. The pain comes from its displacing skin and expanding the tissues, and because of the fluid retention, it is known as "wet beriberi."

In addition to the pain of swelling, there is the more severe pain from direct involvement of the nerves of the toes, feet, and legs. In its pure form, involving the legs without swelling, it is known as "dry beriberi." Most of the prisoners had a combination of the two. I did not know the difference at the time, and subsequently have been told they tend to go together, "wet" favoring severe physical exertion and "dry" favoring relative inactivity. I was starved and inactive after being starved and active; and I struggled with all my body and leg swelling.

Some of those men who had severe leg pain attempted to control the pain by any means possible. They would break the ice off the top of a bucket of water formed in the ambient prison temperature. Because their feet were searing with pain, they placed them in the ice water below. This relieved their pain only temporarily.

I saw them pull their feet out of the water and watched the steam coming off their immersed parts in the frigid barracks, because their feet were warmer to touch than the rest of their body. Yes, they got some pain relief. No, it was not good. They traded in their dry beriberi and got gangrene in return. The flesh would fall off the bones of their toes, and then their bones would be nipped off, under no anesthesia, with some sort of large clippers. They felt no pain. They were ripe for further infection.

I feared this happening to me, so I did not immerse my feet in the ice water. I merely lay in my assigned spot and dreamed of a better day, when this would all be finished. Hour after hour, I still wanted to live through this.

All the prisoners were sitting outside in the sunlight, leaning up against the building because it had warmed from the sun despite the chill in the air on this day, May 7, 1943. The building had no heat, and this was the best way to get a little warm while we picked the lice out of our undergarments.

The important-looking Jap officer with his cheese knife swinging from his resplendent uniform walked up and called everybody to attention. *Ki wo tsuke!* [pronouced "key YOAT ski."]

The Japs had a swaggering gait that made their Samurai swords swing a little more menacingly. This three-and-a-half foot sword I had seen used to decapitate Chinese under their occupation only a few years before. In the military tradition of last century's wars, an officer waving this weapon above his head may have instilled fear in his enemy, but sword waving in World War II was quickly neutralized by a .45 or .03-06 shell. Our GIs thought that such a knife is only good for cutting cheese. With a little imagination, and sometimes it took a very little, one could imagine a cheese-loving rodent displaying the knife. You did not dare smile while thinking this because it would invite a severe beating. Yet I know everybody thought the same thing. Mental telepathy exists. Across our silent sub-vocalization, our collective brain-waves always connected the cheese knife with its rodent owner.

Getting up was hard for us because of the pain and swelling. It took us enough time so that when we stood at attention, his cheese knife had stopped swinging on his hip. We saw boots on him so shiny you could see your reflection in them. He was accompanied by four guards, and began selecting men. I was one of the ten men that he picked out, but we did not know what it was all about.

Then he turned around and departed. The interpreter had gotten our names. They told a British POW doctor, who had been given no medicines or supplies for our benefit, that they intended to do some operation on the ten of us. Apparently they spoke colleague to colleague about the medical aspects of the intended surgery. Hearing their plan, he strenuously objected.

When medical colleagues discuss a procedure, there is sometimes a difference of opinion. Ordinarily, as gentlemen, they discuss the merits of the matter despite professional ranking, but sometimes that can get lively. When the power of the rank was Japanese, and the dissenting opinion was from a British prisoner, the discussion was short.

The Jap guards, representing Jap medicine, merely beat the living hell out of the British opinion presenter.

The British doctor's name was Charles E. Jackson. I will never forget him as long as I live. He was a big man, over six feet tall and had a Van Dyke beard, like the King of England wore back then. Of course, he spoke with a British accent and portrayed the courtly mannerisms. He was quite chipper, but he got beaten to unconsciousness.

On May 10, 1943, our guards loaded us into the back of a dump truck and took us into the hospital in downtown Osaka. At a back door, they unloaded us with great difficulties because of our leg edema and swollen bellies.

A man by the name of Simon McCloud was the first one to receive the operation. He was gone for about an hour and forty-five minutes, and then they came and got me. You were not carried into the operating room by stretcher, you walked.

As I entered the operating room, I saw bloody gauze scattered all around. Simon was lying on the marble floor over in a corner, hurting from the procedure. Bloody instruments were scattered in the tray alongside of the operating table. Used instruments covered the top of a little adjustable table, two legs on one side with wheels and skids adjusted to insert its top over the operating table. I do not know what the Japs called it, but in America it is a Mayo table. This one was dirty, with bloody, used gauze and unclean instruments.

Simon had received some sort of major surgery. I had never seen major surgery or been in a room where it was performed. I had seen my stepfather's office after dental surgery had been performed, and never had I seen gauze sponge wads soaked with blood lying around. This was not a good sign. My thoughts at that time were that nothing was sterile. Left-over sponges from the previous case were lying around to be used on the next patient. I knew I was in deep trouble.

I had carefully hidden my USN tattoos with long-sleeve shirts up to now. Jap culture paints one with tattoos as "bad" or a "gangster." You do not get operated upon with your long-sleeve shirt still on. I sensed even deeper trouble.

They motioned me to get up on the table, and watched as I plumped my swollen body on their table. They smiled, like a cat pawing a half-dead mouse.

Houston, Texas

May 1943 marked an anniversary for my mother. In May 1942, with the surrender of Corregidor, she had become a "Silver Star Mother." The last word she had had was that I was "missing in action," a term that told a parent that her son was not proven to be dead, but not confirmed to be alive. It was one small step above knowing one's son had been killed.

Recognition of mothers who had sons serving in the armed forces came with the placing of a blue star on a field of white bordered in red as a letter-sized flag held in place by a gold braid and tassel. For each son or daughter in the service a blue star was placed in the field of white.

When the War Department of the United States announced that a son was missing in action, the blue star was exchanged for one of silver. When the Western Union Telegraph Boy on bicycle or motorcycle rolled up to your front door with a telegram from the War Department, it generally was not good news. It generally meant that the star you would now display had changed to gold, that color reserved for those who had died in service of their country.

My mother was living with a silver star on her little front window flag.

Half a world away, Jap doctors seemed bent on changing her silver into gold.

Osaka, Japan

I got up on the table. They told me to lie on my left side to give me a spinal anesthetic. I had great difficulties in bowing out my back like a mad cat on a fence, the ordinary posture that opens the space between the bony elements of the spine so that the needle can get into the spinal cord space. My abdomen was very distended from the beriberi, and my thighs and legs were swollen two times their regular size. Bending over to open the spaces for the spinal was next to impossible, but I did the best I could.

When he put the needle in my spinal column, he hit a nerve back there and both my legs shot straight out. The pain was like an electric shock, and I could not control my reaction. Someone grabbed my feet and pushed them back up and the doctor went on with the injection.

I do not know what all they did, for I could not see over my own swollen abdomen. I know that the Jap surgeon and his assistant wore white cotton gloves, like white military inspection gloves, not rubber gloves. These cotton gloves were still soaked from the blood of Simon McCloud, their first patient. From the scar, they did something where my leg joins my abdomen on the right side. The best guess of Navy and civilian doctors years later is that this was some sort of sympathectomy.

When they made the incision into my abdomen, the water gushed out from the beriberi. During starvation, edema fluid collects in the tissue spaces where fat should be. They hit an artesian well and thought that it was so funny. They died laughing because that happened. They might have been conversing in Japanese, but they were laughing in English.

When you are under spinal anesthesia, you are conscious, but the part of the body the doctors are operating on is numb. You cannot feel pain while the spinal lasts. Because you can hear the talk and not understand what they are discussing, it is fearsome. If you heard the talk between English-speaking physicians, you still might not understand the medicalese, but you would know why they were operating and what help they planned to give you.

In this instance, it was medicalese in Japanese from those who did not really care whether you lived or died. Their purpose for operating was not known to me. When that purpose was explained to a British surgeon, he objected and got beaten up. This did not sound right. It didn't sound good. My terror was intense.

The spinal lasted only about thirty minutes. I began to feel some pain from the cutting and pulling. The operation, according to the people that were there, took an hour and forty-two minutes. Simon McCloud had a ringside seat lying on the marble floor and looking up. Though he was passing in and out of consciousness, he saw the spectacle of what happened when my anesthesia prematurely wore off.

With the anesthesia gone, I knew they were trying to kill me. I started trying to get up off the table. They slugged me over my left eye, busting it open at the eyebrow, and slammed me back down on the table.

They gave me some intramuscular injection, for there was no IV going. This stuff made me fade in and out of consciousness for the duration of the procedure.

The Jap butchers were hell-bent on operating, so they did not wait for the injection to take effect. They put a sheet across my chest and tied it across the operating table so I couldn't get up. I was face-up on the table. They went on and finished the operation, whatever it was.

They talked ninety miles an hour in Japanese. I remember the part where they closed the incision. My pain was intense when he roughly grabbed me by my operation's skin flap as his lifting handle hard enough to pull me off the operating table. Had it not been for the tight sheet restraining my chest, I know they would have succeeded. Though they closed their abdominal operation at the end of the procedure, they did not sew up the laceration of my eyebrow. They did bandage it.

They put us in the back of the dump truck that evening and transported all of us back to the prison hospital. You can imagine how much fun it was, riding in the back of a rough empty dump truck after major surgery.

We got back to Ichioka Prison Hospital, where the prisoners unloaded us and put us back onto these bays. We were weak and sore, but we could not get up and do anything.

The British doctor came in to check on us. We never saw the Jap surgeon again. I was running a high temperature, like the other guys who had been operated on, and I figured we all had infections.

There was no medicine for pain in the postoperative period. Once the spinal wore off, the soreness from the cuts, pulls, and all component parts of the surgery were unbearable.

There were no IVs or even pills for pain. An old coffee can became our bedside urinal. A round cedar tub a foot in diameter and four inches high ordinarily used by the Japanese to carry vegetables in from the garden was pressed into use as our bedpan. Medical corpsmen became our nurses.

"Corpsman! Piss tin in four bay!" you yelled when you wanted the nurse. The King's English translation for this was: "Corpsman. Urinal in the fourth bed in the bay of beds."

I do not remember the wording to summon the cedar tub "bedpan." Diarrhea was so prevalent that maybe the guttural predrop grunt was enough to get the tub there, stat! We had regular diarrhea, and some of them had amebic dysentery, distinguishable by smell.

The postoperative care consisted of taking our temperature, feeling the pulse for rate and character. There was no blood pressure taken.

Charles E. Jackson, the British doctor, came at the end of the first week to take my stitches out. When he got to the next-to-the-last stitch, the incision burst wide open, ejecting blood and pus with a smell of rotten eggs down my crotch and leg and onto the mat where I lay.

When the orderlies had finished cleaning me all up, there was a gaping hole approximately seven-and-a-half inches long and three-and-a-half inches wide in my belly. Fortunately my intestines did not protrude. They irrigated the area with plain tap water, not a sterile solution, but obviously a thousand times cleaner than the material that came out.

Each day they would press on the right side of my body to roll me over and catch this rotten drainage in a used powdered-milk can, about the size of a one-pound coffee can. The Red Cross would ship powdered milk to us in these containers, but most were intercepted and the prisoners never got them. Overnight I would fill it up three-quarters of the way, but all was not pus. In addition to discharge from the infection there were fluids from the beriberi. Prior to using the can to capture drainage, it would simply run down between my legs and I would be sitting in a puddle at the end of the day. Then someone would have to change everything I was lying on.

Drainage was accomplished by rolling me over on my side, but they were concerned where all this fluid was coming from. Dr. Jackson took a six-inch probe and inserted it into the right side of my abdomen. He searched around the side of my stomach wall toward the back. The probe slipped away from his touch and went completely out of sight. It disappeared.

"This is where the muscle has pulled away," he said, probing a cavity. "The stitches have rotted, and the muscle is like a rubber band being cut and retracted. It goes all around to the center of your back. The infection has reached all the way around to the center of your back, where the fluid is gathering. Then, after the night, you turn over and flush it out. Meanwhile, we got a lost probe."

He managed to get the probe out by taking a pair of forceps and going down and fishing for it. He found it and got it back out, but that was with me lying there with no anesthetic or anything to calm down either the pain or the anxiety. I'm sitting there watching him do all this! This was a rather unique experience, to say the least.

They had nothing with which to treat the infections. Antibiotic treatments were barely at the sulfanilamide stage; and the old standbys of hydrogen peroxide, potassium permanganate, or alcohol were unavailable. Thus it was that they washed me out with just plain water.

The surgical principle of leaving the wound open was easy, except the area open was so large. It would have been simple if all the open area was merely muscle, but it was not. There was the matter of the peritoneum, the specialized tissue that holds in the guts and separates it in a cavity from surrounding organs. It is tissue that acts as a barrier for the intestines and other organs to limit extension into areas they do not belong. It does not have structural strength to hold back, but strength and integrity where the wall-like strength is supplied by something else. In my case, the muscular walls were open, and it would be a matter of time before the peritoneum would be broken. Infection of the peritoneum is called peritonitis, which even in the modern day of antibiotics can still cause death. In the pre-antibiotic age, it was almost always deadly. Thus it was that they used a "butterfly bandage," not the fancy sterile tape one puts on an incision to align the skin, but they got pieces of material eleven inches wide and three feet long. They made strips on each to lap over each other on top of the incision that pressed my stomach together.

That wasn't worth a damn. The infection was so bad, ruining and soiling everything as it made me stink to high heaven. I was in quite a bit of pain. Ordinarily there is relief of pain after the pus flows out, like when a boil is lanced. This was not the case with me. I had intermittent high fever and pain.

On postoperative day sixteen, the ninth day after the incision burst open, the doctor came in and said, "Take this juice for the relief of pain. It's liquid, and you'll have to drink it, but it will make you sleep."

Oh, man, he didn't have to tell me twice. I didn't know what it was, but I found out later it was liquid opium. One shot of that, and I passed out for the first sleep I'd had in seven nights.

For descriptive purposes in a patient's chart, the day of surgery in a legitimate operation is written "Op Day," or operative day, as a title for the note. Those that follow are titled "POD 1," etc., for postoperative day one, etc. The other guys operated on started dying on POD 4. By POD 6, six of the ten patients were dead.

As we were being treated for our postoperative infections, the usual case load was carried. The major illness was wet beriberi. So much fluid had accumulated within the abdomen of some POWs that they could not breathe properly because the diaphragm, the muscle between their abdomen and chest, would not descend. Their rapid and shallow breathing became a life threat. To remedy this, a needle was inserted into the abdominal cavity and the fluid drained. The needle was sterilized with hot water, attached to a rubber hose and pushed into the abdominal cavity. Often times, a half gallon of greenish fluid came out, green from bile. Sometimes the fluid foamed up and looked like dark beer with a head on it, but unlike beer, it was sticky.

They did not do this to me. They wanted to keep everything out of my peritoneal cavity, for only that thin membrane separated the clean gut cavity from all the germs and infections a millimeter away. My infection was located in the tissue below the skin cut and in the spaces left by the retracted muscles. Fortunately, it was not in the peritoneal compartment containing the bowel. The infection did not advance, but the cut area was not healing together.

The external bandages had failed to assist my incision to begin the mending process. My skin was overstretched from the edema caused by the beriberi. It was in poor shape to grow back together, and I did not have the nutrition from my limited diet to promote adequate healing. Something had to be done if I was going to have a chance at surviving.

At this time, the British doctor, Jackson, came in and said, "Kiddie, we're going to have to sew you up." Most Americans called me "Kidd," but he called me "Kiddie."

"Kiddie, we're gonna hafta sew you up," he repeated in the King's English. "Otherwise, you're gonna die."

"Well, okay," I said.

"So we got three problems," he said.

"What's that?"

"One, we don't have anything to do it with. But," he paused, "we've got a needle like you sew your clothes with. We got some black cotton thread. We got some shirt buttons. We'll use that to suture you up."

I probably nodded in the affirmative. What else could I have done?

"But the second problem." He paused again. "You're gonna hafta help."

"What can I do?"

"You're going to have to suck in your stomach wall so the needle head will not perforate the stomach wall and get the infection inside of your abdomen there down into your stomach. Otherwise, you will die." He used simple terms for the bodily areas.

"Awwh. Okay."

"And the third problem." He took a long pause. "We have no anesthetic."

Imagine lying there with no anesthetic and being sewn up with a straight needle and thread. While the doctor used forceps inside to push at the eye-end of the needle through the swollen, edematous subcutaneous tissue and skin atop, the needle was only a thread longer than the tissue thickness. Beriberi and starvation had given me fluid-laden tissue. I would look down and my belly skin would be puckered up; the needle unable to stab through. He could push on the forceps holding at the needle eye with one hand, and with his other thumb and index finger straddle the needle point tenting up my skin. With a combination of tenting-up, pushing down, and needle screwing, it finally stabbed through. He would tell me to suck in my stomach, and I would try to pull my stomach in. It hurt a lot, but neither of us wanted him to stab the peritoneum or intestines enclosed below.

He kept hollering, "Pull it in. Pull it in." And when he got the needle through the skin, he put it through both eyes of a shirt button, and left the end long and loose.

"Blimey!" he said. "You got the toughest hide I ever saw on a man."

It may have been tough, but part of the problem was that he was using a an ordinary sewing needle for suturing the skin. The common sewing needle is straight, round, and comes to a point. It's great for passing between and parting the woven threads of cloth, its thin roundness gliding easily through a shirt, but such a needle does not pass well through skin. Dermal cells resist piercing by tightly closing around any intruder. This was made more difficult because the needle shaft was slippery with my body fluids. At least the British surgeon's fingerprints gave him some traction. He had no gloves to use.

Ordinary surgical skin closure is done by a "cutting needle," one not drawn to a single round tip, but a triangular configuration with three sharp edges coming together at the point. As the apex leads the three edges through the compacted dermal cells, it easily pierces. The surgical cutting needle is a half-circle wire, point on one end with an eye to thread on the other, perfect for grasping with the needle holder, an instrument shaped like a tiny needle-nosed pliers with finger loops on each handle. These two simple suturing tools were not available to the British surgeon.

"Blimey!"

On the opposite side, he likewise pushed the same needle through my subcutaneous tissue and skin from the inside of the wound out. After stabbing through, he looped the thread through the two eyes of another shirt button and let the loose end lie free on top. The lowest stitch had been placed, its two buttons waiting to be tied; but not until five more stitches equally spaced above it had been placed. Then there were six stitches in for the length of the wound, twelve buttons on six black cotton shirt threads, untied, but in.

With a couple of assistants pushing the Jap-made incision toward the mid-line to take the tension off until after all six had been tied, they released slowly. *Yes!* It held, giving me a double-breasted skin suit.

I could not keep from coughing as he operated, thus making a moving target for him, but he finally finished after so many hours. The button bolsters kept the cotton threads between them barely off my skin so they would not simply slice through. In time, skin between the buttons suffered some cross-cutting from the threads, but the buttons-and-stitches arrangement held me together. The slow process of healing began.

From that day forward, I was called "Buttons" in Ichioka, the prison where they expected you to die. I lay there, unable to get up. I had a cold, and my coughing inadvertently tested Dr. Jackson's sutures. Eventually the threads pulled through the skin tissue, but by then the wound started to close from the inside out, a lengthy process, called "secondary intention" by surgeons.

It took months for this hole in my abdomen to fill with scar tissue. It had to fill from the bottom up, not from top down or from side to side or end to end. Each month you could see that the bottom of the wound had risen and the cavity was a little shallower. The discharge became less onerous in its odor, less purulent in its character, and smaller in its volume. A scab formed and healing took place beneath. I had the definite feeling I would live and, perhaps someday, not smell like a dozen rotten eggs.

In the meantime, they used a butterfly-type bandage to help hold in my abdomen and support my privates to where I could get up. I had to learn to walk all over again. After six months of total inactivity, I had no control over moving my legs. With the aid of the other prisoners to support me, I was able to move about. Then I managed to get a stick—not a walking cane, but a stick—to help support myself. I wanted to be as independent as possible.

I was no speed demon, but I got some exercise. The rallying cry as I walked a mile in three and a half hours was "Here comes Buttons."

As my tissues healed together inside, the shirt thread on top near the buttons cut the skin. This irritation was relieved months later, when my mending tissues were stronger and the stitches came out. As I lost my need for the buttons, my nickname faded.

Thirty-six kilograms was approximately my weight at that time. At 2.2 pounds per kilogram, I weighed about eighty pounds. I was not at what you would call "fighting strength," but I was alive.

I got a chance one day to go out and sit in the sun at the stadium. There I spotted a large clump of clover growing in the ground. When the guard was not looking, I sat down beside the clover and decided it looked good enough to eat. Only the rain had washed it, and I had three hands full. Needless to say, I had a problem with diarrhea after that, but it was the first greenery I had eaten in over two and a half years. Believe it or not, clover is not all that bad.

Though I had witnessed the British doctor's beating before my surgery, I did not know what it was about until later. The Japs were always beating up on someone for one reason or another, or for no reason at all. You dared not even cast your eyes toward them with an inkling of a question. That kind of look could get you beaten or killed. The British doctor had been punished for voicing his distrust and disagreement about the operations being performed on the prisoners. Why they informed him is unknown, for they did not care whether he approved or not. Those experiments were done at the whim of the Jap doctors.

Dr. Jackson told me that, excluding the damaged done by the infection and beriberi, the intent by this Jap doctor was to do a sympathectomy. What else was done, he had no idea; but it was strictly an experimental operation to see what effect it would have on the beriberi.

In the day and time the operation was performed on me, sympathectomies were performed by a posterior incision, an incision on the back to get to the dorsal nerve roots and sympathetic nerve outflow. I am told that the first one was performed by an Australian surgeon in 1924 in that manner. Today, the preferred approach is the anterior approach, like mine was done.

Whether my operation was the general approach used in Japanese sympathectomies, whether he wanted to be on the cutting edge of a surgical procedure change, or whether the Jap doctor needed to acquire some "animal lab experience" before working on Japanese patients is unknown. It is not uncommon for a surgeon to perform some new procedure on laboratory animals to hone his skills for humans.

Perhaps, in the Bushido tradition as interpreted by this physician, he would personally benefit from some "lab rat" operations on "white mice"; only these "white mice" were two-legged white-skinned American GIs. These "animals" were about to die anyway and, consequently, of no value to the Emperor. It may be that the doctor, who I am told was later transferred to the infamous Camp 731, was using us as his initiation for entrance to that place of dishonor. Who knows? When a third of your friends and acquaintances die of starvation and beatings, you are not likely to conclude there was much honor in the residents of the Rising Sun.

Although I began to get more strength, I still weighed in as the puny "ninety pound weakling" of the Charles Atlas ads of the day. I could not gain any weight because there was no food to eat.

The Jap theory was that the working man got most of the food. If you did not work, or you did a clerical job, you got less food than the laborer. The sick individual got half what the clerk got. The person doing heavier labor was fed just enough so that his death would come slower and he could work longer. We were practically starving to death the whole time we were supposed to be healing.

Sometime around July 1944, I was advised that I was going to be transferred near the waterfront for "limited duty" at the Osaka headquarters camp.

I got down there by truck and I quickly found out that this was a slave work camp where the prisoners serviced many industries. There was stevedore work unloading ships at the dock area or barges, working in the steel mills, loading trains, and unloading supplies and goods from the warehouses. The primary concern we worked for was Sumatoma, for which we were paid a fee. Sumatoma paid us at the rate of three yen per month. A pack of cigarettes with ten to the pack sold for three yen, so the guys bought a pack a month.

The job they had in mind for us to do when we arrived was referred to in Japanese as *byoki* [bee OH key], which means "sick people." Byoki performed light duties, like paperwork. I was assigned to fold printed Jap propaganda leaflets for two weeks in the room with other byoki, and I was still fed a light diet.

However, I was fortunate enough to be in this camp where the POWs had access to extra food out on the job, which they would steal and prepare. When it came time to get their ration at night back at the base camp barracks, I was with the guys that were working on these stevedoring jobs. They would give me half or their entire evening food ration because they had eaten on the job before they came in. I thought I had died and gone to heaven because I had not seen this much rice since the wartime activities had started in the Philippines. I could have a whole bowl of rice of my own issue, and they would give me all the additional rice I could eat. I finally started regaining some weight and strength.

A month later, I was advised by our barracks captain that he was trying to get me a job as a cook on a work crew. The lunch meal for the working crews was a Japanese issued *bento*, which consisted of a rice patty and one pickled daikon slice. Sometimes, in lieu of the daikon, they got seaweed. These men who performed the heavy labor jobs needed more than just rice for nourishment. They had to stay in better shape than most of the prisoners and needed a cook out on the job site to cook the usual Jap fare plus whatever edibles they were able to steal from the warehouses. This included rice, soybeans, and dried fish when they could find it.

Of course, our Jap civilian guard, the *Joshi* [HON-cho], knew that we were doing this. In fact, they often ate some of it themselves. Whatever the prisoners brought in I would cook. I cooked up the rice in a five-gallon can over an open fire to which sometimes we added dried salmon. The nourishment in those instances was tremendous compared to the usual meals.

We also worked in the Sumatoma warehouse, where they had various things stored, including shoes, clothing, and canned fruits.

One of the worst beatings I ever got happened after I had been tipped off by one guy who said, "Hey, Kidd, they found some canned tangerines in the back of this warehouse. They're stacked behind a pile of hundred-kilo rice bags. All you got to do is climb up there. It's easy. Just come around when the guard isn't looking and climb up there and find the case. Open up the cans right there and eat you some tangerines. Then, just put the empty can back in the case and close the box back up." When all the tangerines had been eaten and the case was empty, whoever loaded it onto the train pretended the case was still heavy.

I ate tangerines for two days. On the third day, I got caught. The guard walked up on me while I was up there eating a can of tangerines. He started kicking me, and I started rolling down the bags of soybeans and rice. The guard ran behind me, kicking me all the way down until I finally hit the concrete floor.

"Get up! Get up!" the guys hollered at me. Most of the Japs preferred to knock you down repeatedly, but if you stayed down, they might shoot you. Of course, I was trying to protect my operative site as well as my head. He kicked me in my back, neck, and buttocks.

I finally got up on my feet, and all he was screaming to me was, *Gangu! Gangu!* which means "gangster." Chicago gangster.

I definitely got the impression that the word meant I was bad, because I had been caught stealing a can of those tangerines the Japs had previously stolen from some conquered country. He beat me mercilessly. After he had finished pummeling me, he went on about his business and I went back to my duty of cooking for the crew. I learned not to be caught after that. I kept a quick eye out for anything that might be approaching me. From that time on, every time the guard saw me, he would call me *Gangu.* The guard never did know the nickname of "Buttons"; to him I was *Gangu.*

The sleeping quarters were situated in the center of the camp, and work crews were sent out to various points daily. We had the crew that worked in the steel mill area, the warehouse, and several distribution points where ships and trains were loaded or unloaded. Lower-class Japanese civilians, perhaps one step above the coolie, were in charge of the work details and assigned our duties each day. These were the *Joshio*, which is Japanese for "boss."

For some unknown reason, the crew that worked at the steel mill was able to trade with the Japanese for cigarettes. Cigarettes were plentiful at the steel mill, but since we had no money, we had to barter. For example, sugar and shoes were highly prized premium products. During the war, both were unavailable from the stores. Our crews were working with these commodities on a daily basis. It would be a matter of taking the product out of the Jap military pipeline and putting it into the Japanese civilian pipeline.

We set up a bartering system whereby we supplied them with a certain amount of sugar, shoes, or clothing, and they supplied us with cigarettes. The market existed, but there was the matter of exchanging supplies without getting killed for doing so.

Each morning the military guards mustered us at the barracks for the *tenko* (roll call) and *bango* (count off) before sending us out on work details. The steel mill detail rode in a truck because of the distance. Those that worked on the Sumatoma warehouse were within marching distance from the camp, so they marched off in the morning and back in the evening.

Most of the trading material was acquired from the Sumatoma warehouse. The warehouse details had to steal the stuff, conceal it, and then smuggle it back into the camp. There, it was passed to the crews, who were going out to the steel mill the next morning. These people had to take it from the camp to the steel mill and deliver it to the Japanese civilians out there. The Japanese civilians, in turn, paid for the goods with cigarettes, which would have to be hidden and brought back into the camp. The cigarettes would be used to pay off the crew that had brought the sugar, shoes or clothing.

It was vicious bartering between the various details in the camp versus the Japanese. We ran one of the best black markets in Japan. I watched guys bring in as much as sixty pounds of sugar while standing in line for inspection by the Jap guards. They accomplished this by simply tying up the long johns at their ankles and filling the legs full of sugar. Some put sugar in socks and lay it across their upper torso or across their shoulders and down their back. If the guards found anything on you, they punished you brutally for the next two or three days. You stood at attention with no food, and then you were beaten.

The barter express was done on a regular basis, at least two or three times a month. Sometimes we would bring in dried salmon. The materials we acquired were merely the materials the Japs had stolen from their captured islands and territories for consumption in the Japanese homeland. The ability of the prisoners in that particular camp to procure this merchandise the way we did, I feel, enabled us to survive our crude conditions of existence.

Eleven

To Fetch a Pail of Water

The one item of top priority in Japan that made no sense to us at the time was soap. None of us knew enough of their culture to understand about communal bathing and their passion for cleanliness. From our personal experience, dirt was deemed their way of life.

Soap was one of the highest-priced articles in Japan. Somewhere in their conquests in China, the Philippines, and the South Pacific islands, the Japs came across a lot of U.S. Navy Salt Water Soap. Bars eighteen-inches long by two and a half inches square, dense and heavy for their size, were a staple on all U.S. Navy ships. In prison camp we were given shaved-off little pieces about the size of today's hotel hand soap. It would have to last the entire month for all our washing, bathing, and laundry needs.

One day, a prisoner crew working for Sumatoma was sent on a detail unloading cases of their captured soap from a barge. In Japan, families lived in private quarters on one end of the barge. For some unknown reason, the family on this one was absent when the crew unloaded its content. When the prisoners were pulled off the detail before it was completely unloaded, a scheme was hatched to reacquire our naval cleaning stores.

We had some latitude to walk about unguarded without arousing suspicion because we were working in several warehouses at a time. A group together would not be missed at work nor would they be questioned while walking along unguarded—certainly not a group that looked intent on carrying out their assigned duties.

Six of the prisoners slipped away from their current detail and went down to the canal, where they had been unloading the soap. They stole the barge by manually hauling it up the canal to a new mooring place, then tried to hide it. There was, however, one problem with the whole operation. When the family came back from their trip, their barge with their living quarters was gone. They were as upset as anyone might be coming home to find their whole house stolen.

There was a lot of jabbering in Japanese among the family that lived on the barge, the guards, and the *Joshi.* We had no idea what had taken place, until we were informed that the barge had been stolen, the cargo included. The barge was approximately forty feet long and nine feet wide at the beam. To move that thing in water took some kind of power, but these men did it

Upon our return to camp that evening, the guards questioned everyone there about it, and nobody knew a darn thing. They stood us at attention and we all got frisked. The Jap guards conducted a careful body search, and of course, they didn't find any soap.

They did find a sock full of sugar on one guy and beat him without mercy. The sugar was not like the white sugar we use on the tables today, but a brown, unrefined sugar. They beat that fellow as if he alone possessed sugar, the missing soap, and the stolen barge.

They brought the interpreter out and questioned everybody. We still denied everything, so they stood us up for five hours at attention in front of the guard shack. The guards scrutinized us for anyone who kind of slumped down instead of standing at rigid attention. The guard would slap you upside the head hard enough to knock you down. This lasted well into the early-morning hours, until we were finally told that they had found the barge. Then they let us go to the barracks. We managed to sleep a couple of hours before reveille and regular work time.

We found out that six guys had moved the barge, and they were going to stash it away where they could steal the soap for our bartering trade. Unfortunately they lost their chance.

I was part of a work detail that took us away from our camp each day for about a month, placing me near my original entrance to Japan, Camp Yodogawa Bunsho. I saw some of the men working at the steel mill across the canal and started hollering at them. A guard came up from my blind side and bopped me upside the head hard enough to knock me down. I didn't even know he was behind me. He stood over me and snarled something in Japanese. I took it to mean I was to shut up and get back to work.

I never could do the work the rest of the guys did because I didn't have the physical ability due to my operation. The other POWs, the non-operated-on ones who had only our common bondage of starvation, beatings, and lice, did my share of the lifting along with theirs. I was the chief cook and bottle washer on the job and prepared any stolen food they were able to find to add to our rations.

On the steel-mill detail, we stacked fifty-five-gallon steel drums, which gave us nothing to steal. How do you get a fifty-five-gallon empty drum by the guards, and who would want one? The only good thing about the steel-mill detail was the availability of cigarettes. Our work detail would smuggle sugar stolen elsewhere out to that location and trade the sugar to the Japs for cigarettes. How and where they got the cigarettes, I have no idea. It was really strange because the Japs on our other details could not get cigarettes.

On this one particular early spring day, the detail was stacking these fifty-five-gallon empty drums in long rows laying flat on their sides, ten high at the top level point. The pile was the height of the roof ridge line on an ordinary two-story house. A "stairway of drums" went from ground level to top, with three sets of guys from the ground to the top. Two guys standing at the lower level of the stairway took a drum and swung it between them. They would toss it up to two guys farther up the "stairway," who would toss it to the next two until it came to the two on top. The limitation was how high two guys could toss it up to the next two. It was amazing to see it done.

As we were at a pier admiring our neatly stacked marvel, an earthquake hit. Though I had experienced earth tremors in California and Manila, my first full-blown earthquake was in Japan. The earth started moving, and I looked up and saw that the drums were beginning to shake. The POWs on the steel drums were scrambling to get down. The earth was moving with such a force that you couldn't stand up. I sat down.

About that time, the ground near the stack of drums opened up at the water line, and the two-story-high stack of drums sank ten feet below ground level. Water from a rainfall the night before sloshed out of the puddles. Hot steam and boiling water came shooting out of the ground about forty feet into the air like a geyser. I had never in my life seen anything like that, and it scared the living daylights out of me. I thought, *It's a helluva a note to die this way.*

I looked around at the steel mill's hundred-feet-tall concrete smokestacks that usually stood stiffly at attention in stately rows. During the quake, these smoke stacks danced strangely, creating "Xs" in the sky as they wobbled out of their parallel lines. The stacks did not crumble, but merely bypassed each other while dancing, before returning to their original positions.

The quake finally subsided. Thank God, it didn't last long. Some of the buildings around us had fallen, but luckily we were out in the open. On the ride home that evening, we saw a lot of damage in the various housing areas between Osaka and Kobe.

Having seen such devastation to the civilian area, we figured we would be sleeping out in the open that night, but our camp was unharmed. As rough as it was at our job site, an area that had been filled with dirt debris, cinders, and rocks to reclaim land from the sea for this plant, our camp was unharmed.

I was put out on a work detail aboard ship, and I was able to carry my weight in assigned duties there because I ran the winch. Hell, I'd never run a winch in my life. As an onlooker, I had seen someone else run one before, but the Japs had ordered me to run theirs. I knew better than to argue with them.

I knew what to do with a throttle to pick up a load, and how to let it back down, so we unloaded soy beans out of the ship's hold into a barge on the side. The POWs lifted 100-Kg (220-pound) bags of soybeans and set fifteen bags into a two-strap sling. The sling rings would be looped on a winch hook, and the winch would lift it up out of the hold. After getting it to a height to clear other objects on the ship, I would swing it out over the side of the ship down to the barge for the other POWs to unload.

The soy beans were enclosed in loose burlap bags that looked like big pillows with four corners. Two POWs using "coggies" handled the bags in an ingenious manner shown them. A coggie has a wooden handle looking like someone has molded a golf ball into the shape of a large Hershey's

Kiss, and extruding from its point is a J-shaped pencil-sized steel rod that tapers down to a needle point.

With one coggie in each hand, the men would hook their points into the burlap bag's pouty corners, the point readily separating the fibers. The duo would bend forward, hook the two nearest corners, and lean backwards at the same time. Using their body weight, it was easy to lift the bag chest-high. Another man would stoop over and scoot under as the two put it down on his shoulders. The stooped man unflexed his knees and walked away with the bag as the two disengaged their four coggies. Occasionally a bean or two toppled out.

Two coggies in the same bag ear made a better hole for bean spillage, and, better yet, left no tear in the bag as the fibers snapped back in place. Thus a lot of loose soy beans were available, but the uncooked soy bean is very hard to eat. Seeing all this, I thought, there has to be a way to cook soy beans.

It looked like a navy bean, and when cooked, was tasty, high in protein. The Japs hated them mixed in their *bento*, their noon lunch of rice rations, and would take them out and toss them away. We retrieved them, but we needed a way to cook beans onboard ship.

"Well, I got it figured out," I said one day. "On the steam winch, you've got a cylinder drum that operates off steam to go back and forth in order to drive the wheel, similar to the old steam locomotive engine. This turning wheel winds the cable, which picks up the load."

A petcock valve on the drum where steam goes in exists to open in case of an emergency from excessive steam pressure. Considering steam as hot water under pressure, I took a canteen cup of beans tucked away in a piece of tow sack and attached them to the petcock. I poked a hole in the cloth with the petcock spout and tied the sacked cup of beans to the valve stem, cracking the petcock slightly open. Live steam readily cooked those beans.

I would sit there and run that winch until I thought they were done. Then I would get down and open it up to check. If they were soft, I would take them; and if not I'd run it some more. We were loading the barges while cooking our lunch.

When it came time to take a break and get our *bento,* we also had these *soy beans a la steam winch* which tasted good and helped us to survive because of the protein we were able to get.

Our four working winches periodically required cleaning, so the Japs used an oil-based cleaning compound. It got into the steam and was transferred to our beans. On cleaning days, it destroyed the flavor of the beans, our first taste screaming that they were unfit to eat. On regular days, the beans were good.

We had not seen any meat in three years—none! I think in that three-year period I saw fish carcasses two or three times. Hell, you ate bones and all. You crushed them up with your teeth and ate the fish bone meal. You didn't throw anything away. That was the extent of our meat. Rice, the daikon soup, and some occasional seaweed composed our diet. One can readily see why we all suffered from beriberi and pellagra.

On March 13, 1945, at about eight o'clock at night, we came under attack by ship-based aircraft from the U.S. Navy carriers operating offshore Osaka. The hour-long attack was memorable because it represented the first actual bombings in our immediate area. We'd seen the B-29s go over so high you could hardly tell they were there. First you would locate the vapor trail, and then you would look ahead a distance and pick out a little speck at the front. You could not hear them. They flew so high that nothing could get to them. No *ack-ack.* Nothing. We stared in wonderment that something could fly that high. We dared not cheer, for it took so little to make our waspish guards mad; and our guys were too high to hear us.

The Navy attack of March 13th was different. They came in at such a low altitude, we knew they were Navy planes. Our camp was not marked in any way, shape, or form as a POW camp, and thus we were indistinguishable from any other cog in Tojo's war machine. From the fires started by bombing, we could read the numbers on the planes. We dared not cheer. Outside the camp buildings we stood with our mouths flung wide open. That is all the guards saw.

Inside the barracks we were silently and discreetly slapping each other on the backs and smiling, especially the Navy flight crew and pilot POWs. Outside, we cheered, with our eyes heavenward, at these planes. You could read "Navy" on the side of the fuselage. We thought, *Boy, they're right off shore and are gonna land right here tonight!* But that did not happen.

They did considerable damage. Thank God, they didn't drop at the shore line or they would have gotten us. They did bomb inland beyond us, and consequently the fires were as bright as day.

That night the family of the camp's Sergeant Major was wiped out in the bombing raid. Consequently we had some serious problems to deal with the next day when we were getting ready to go to work

At the *bongo,* the morning muster, he went down the line with a question to us in Japanese.

He wanted to know, *A-coco* or *Bay coco*? American or British?

The Americans in the front line got the hell slapped out of them; the British were left alone. By the end of his trip down the first of the line, the majority of the camp seemed to be *Bay coco,* but he beat quite a few guys that were standing in the front ranks.

There were four or five roll calls of the POWs each day. They were wake up, detail counting, detail counting prior to return to camp, muster by guards upon arriving at camp, and at the end of the day would be *tenko.* Morning *bongo* before work and *tenko* helped to make us proficient in counting in Japanese. You had to muster at night in the barracks to make sure everyone was there. These musters were really useless, but it let the Japs keep a close accounting of all the prisoners. Because we were mostly Caucasians in Japan, there was no way that anyone could escape and get away with it. We stood out like sore thumbs, so escape was out of the question. No place to go, nobody to hide you, no way of getting out to sea to meet any of your ships. We probably would have been blown out of the water if we tried it. How could they know it was Americans? Believe me, escape was not tried. We decided to ride it out until the war was over and hopefully get with our troops again.

Cleanliness in our camp was practically nonexistent. We had no showers or any way to take a bath. You took your bath out on the work detail after you got finished with work. That was usually supplied by a fire hose of nonheated water, out in the open and at the edge of a building somewhere, hopefully in the sunshine.

Once a month they might take you into a regular, heated public bathhouse for a bath. Since they did not change water after the first half of us bathed, the second half merely exchanged their dirt. Our lice tended to stay safely tucked away in our clothing during these baths, perhaps relishing their freshly washed "food."

I do not remember ever seeing a shower or anything that resembled one. You washed your clothing on the job as well. We had two sets of clothing, one to wear and one in reserve, stored in your bunk, which had been upgraded to a mat on wooden-slat shelves with one horse blanket.

Everyone had lice. They were your buddies, and their favorite places of residence were the creases and seams of your clothing. They slipped out from these places to bite. It was one of these buddy deals. You eat and you feed them. We also had some of the biggest bedbugs I had ever seen in my life. However, this was the *only* time in my life I'd seen a bedbug. I call them "bedbugs," but in reality they were brown ticks. I have seen ticks from my dairy-farm days in Texas, but these Jap bugs were a lot larger, about the size of your little fingernail. After the lights went off, they would come out from the wooden slats you slept on, and from the posts that supported the slats. You would wake up the next morning, and your ankles would be itching from their bites. If you mashed one, the rank tick stench stayed in the air for days. To put it bluntly, they were everywhere in the buildings.

A passageway down in between the bed shelves of the barracks straddled a twenty-four-inch-wide table going the full length of the barracks. You could sit down on the end of the table if you had a reason to sit there.

The tiers that you crawled into to sleep had enough space between you and the next tier so that when the guard walked in the doorway and yelled, "*Ki wo Tsuke*" [key OAT skee], you mustered sitting up in your bunk. After the "attention" command had been completed, he yelled, "*Bongo.*" At this time you counted in a numerical order, different from your prisoner number. I was usually number seventy-one. This could be a variable number depending upon who might have died up or down the line, so it was imperative you know your numbers in Japanese.

My prison number was 684—in Japanese, *roppyaku-hachiju-yon ban.* [Roka-hockey-hock-a-JEW-Yawn] I haven't forgotten it, and I can still count off in Japanese.

Because there was a number for your presence in your bunk that was different from your prison number, you were learning two numbers in Japanese. This was extremely difficult for some of the prisoners, so we helped each other. As the sound-off came down the line like a verbal wave. If your buddy sitting next to you had forgotten his number, you would quickly whisper it to him before he had to sound off. Numbering went the whole line for the lower tier and then went up to the next tier. Your number was generally the same every night. Mine was *Nanaju Ichi* [Hatchie Itchie], 71. The guards did not try to trip you up, but they were clearly serious that it be done properly.

One of our prime concerns was news about the war. For us, there was none. On June 1, 1945, I was working with a detail of some eighty-five men off-loading barges from ships offshore. The barges were getting few and farther between. Those who went out to work on the ships could see the visible machine-gun hits where they had been strafed. We knew the Americans had a task force operating off shore out there somewhere to give that kind of damage. As the ships in Osaka Harbor became fewer, the barge work trailed out to just about none, and our details had us concentrating on these warehouses.

We heard the wail of the air-raid sirens go off, and our *Joshi* came running to tell us that the B-29s were coming.

"Okay," we said. We had seen them come in and pass over many times before.

"No, no, no," said the *Joshi*. "They come *here*."

I wondered how in the hell they would know where they were coming. Surely, our side wouldn't publicize it. But, in reality, they did. The Air Force actually dropped leaflets and told them they were going to bomb a specific area, and to clear out the civilians. That is where they would bomb.

When they hit us on June 1st, there were two hundred and fifty B-29s that attacked Osaka. They came in west of us and started dropping bombs at the water's edge, right where we were.

We watched them come over at about 14,000 feet. We could literally see the bombs leaving the open bomb-bay doors at the bottom of the plane. Never before had we seen B-29s up this close. The biggest thing we had ever seen before that was a B-17, before we were captured. These B-29s looked like houses and had wingspans like football fields. We watched twenty-seven bombers flying in V-formation with our mouths hanging open. I flashed back to memories of another bomber squadron in V-formation, years ago, Japs coming at us from Manila Bay, "meatballs" on their wings . . . but this one was beautiful.

We wanted to cheer, but you would get stuck with a bayonet if you did. So we did not show any emotion, other than fear about getting bombed. Lo and behold, the next flight was an overlapping bombing pattern.

The next flight dropped incendiaries as well as a few two-hundred-and-fifty-pounders. The incendiaries were in cartridges approximately four inches in diameter by thirty inches long, filled with napalm. The heavy end would hit the ground first and blow the napalm out. As soon as the napalm hit the air, it would incinerate. Cement buildings would burn like paper. Those napalm canisters were strung out all around us. You could not take a regulation thirty-six-inch step without stepping on one. Those canisters hit everywhere, and the whole place was ablaze.

We started running, and the Jap guards tried to get us back to camp. We were five miles south of our camp, and he was trying to get us to run back in that direction. We were running towards the next site of pattern bombing. If we had stayed where we were, we would have been safer.

When we heard those bombs come down, it sounded like a bed sheet ripping. That sound was not really different from the Jap bombs back in Corregidor. You knew they were on top of you when you heard that ripping sound. Then you felt the boom.

We ran two miles down the street, double-timing with our guards when we had to take cover from the bombing raids. "Taking cover" meant we fell flat on the street near a curb, hugging the ground to let the blast go by.

We were in the cement warehouses when this hundred-pound thing went through the roof, to the second deck, and down to the first floor, where we were. It looked like a nose plate of an incendiary bomb but did not explode, thank God. Those napalm canisters were on the outside, and the building we were in was burning. We had to go back outside, where the Japanese were running down the street. This one individual had a mattress that he was carrying. He had gripped the sides of it with each hand and pulled it around him. The back of the mattress was ablaze, and he was running down the street with it held up over him. I guess that was his prized possession.

We were very fortunate. Six hundred and forty-four men out of seven hundred were out working that day. Our camp had been zeroed in on, and it burnt to the ground. There was no more camp, but no one was seriously hurt in that bombing raid. All the guys on our detail had survived it. We spit up black goo and coughed from the napalm smoke. The fumes tasted and smelled like gasoline. Everything was burnt. We had nothing left but what we were wearing.

We were delivered over to another camp in the Osaka area that had been a shipbuilding plant. It had been evacuated previously because of bombing attacks. There we were, sitting back in the bull's eye in this camp. You could see the craters where the bombs had been dropped. They were not incendiaries. These were high-explosive craters that were fifteen feet across where the bombs had gone down and blown out all of the dirt. Bomb holes filled with green water. We went through a lot of air raids, and fortunately, none hit us right on. They hit right around us, but I say the good Lord was looking out for us; we had been in the middle of the bull's-eye in both places.

An all-afternoon train ride with our guards to the upper-north end of Honshu took us to our new camp called Aomori, three and a half miles beyond the town proper. We were the only group of POWs in this camp, which was two miles from the waterfront. A river ran into this secluded bay separated from the ocean by a narrow opening where a submarine net gave them absolute security. The only entrance or exit was through this tight enclosure.

This is where ships that got through were unloaded, after Osaka had been bombed beyond usefulness. We were told that we were going to be unloading ships up there, all types of ships. Not content with forcing us to unload food and supplies, the Japs wanted the prisoners to unload ammunition ships.

Our protests and Geneva Convention reminders fell on the deaf ears of our new captors.

"Hey, that's bad news," our chief informed them with a wry face. The narrow eyes of the inscrutable Orientals questioned. "Because there's some one of these 'patriotic jerks' out here among us that's gonna set one of those things off. Then you're not gonna have any ship, any slaves, or anybody left, because they'll blow it all up. You people need to think about that."

I don't know whether that would have occurred to them or not, but the Chief Petty Officer's bluster at least convinced them that it was possible. So we did not have to unload any ammunition. We did unload other perishable goods, like the beans, and rice.

We were very bombing conscious at that time. We had been bombed continuously, every day since Osaka, everywhere we moved. So we asked our new guards, "When's the last time you've been bombed?"

"Never," they answered, "we haven't been bombed during the whole war."

"Man," I said, "we're lucky. We finally got to where we are safe."

The third day we were there, the Americans bombed it. Then we said, "Man, that monkey's riding right on our shoulder."

They came over at night, but they didn't hit us. Not much of anything was hit. It was unlike the usual bombing runs we had been involved in.

The river flowing from the mountains was a fast-flowing rush of water into the protected bay as we were marched to the dock area the next morning.

Shortly thereafter, heavy explosions rocked several ships. Everyone was looking up in the air trying to see the bombers. There were no bombers in sight.

We all thought that a submarine must have gotten past the net and fired torpedoes at the anchored ships in the harbor. They brought in all the sub-chasers they had, and they were running back and forth out there *pinging* for all they were worth. The raid on the ships was brazen enough to be in broad daylight while the sub-chasers were scouring the bay looking for them. They were unable to find any sub or spot where one might have come in through the net.

The planes had made their raid at night on their way to somewhere else, and the subs hit the next day but could not be found. This situation bothered the Japs as well as us. If you are in the "Bull's-Eye," you want to know.

The next day after the ships were attacked, the Japs found something in the mud flats of the river. It looked like a couple of fifty-gallon drums had been welded together. They thought it looked more like a "mine" than a "bomb" and, upon closer inspection, determined it was. The Japs realized that this "mine" came from those planes that flew over. Our guys dropped magnetic mines in the deepest part of the river that got carried down by the currents out to the bay. They floated below the surface, and as current passed by the ships, they exploded on contact. These were the "torpedoes" from the "submarines" on the safe side of the net.

You talk about accuracy—in my estimation, this was the ultimate in accuracy at night. Those huge bombers had placed those mines in that river and let them float. Once in the river, there was little chance of missing one of the cargo ships because they were tied up so close together you could walk from one side of the bay to the other on the decks of ships.

In the first part of August, the autumn weather arrived. We got up each morning to march from our camp into town. Two hundred yards from our camp was an antiaircraft battery sitting right at our back door.

"Boy," I said, "we're still in the bull's-eye."

Our job was at the waterfront. Several days after the mine explosion, I carried a pail up the hill from our slave-labor area where intact faucets supplied enough water to cook paltry rice for our crew after the previous night's bombing. Motley underweights exhibiting the ravages of beriberi and pellagra—fatal diseases of malnutrition long ago wiped out back home—we, the survivor serfs, had been "guests of the Emperor of Japan" for three years.

My mind was absorbed in mundane matters, like how to carry water in the pail without spilling it. The ever-present Jap guards, spoiling to slap an American POW for any real or imagined minor infraction, had perfected their vocation. You focused silently on the menial. The background work buzz punctuated by Nipponese approached eleven o'clock when suddenly things felt different. An awkward serenity descended on the workplace. All the Japanese stood silently with their heads bowed. I started listening.

My ability to understand Japanese was not all that sharp, but I knew a few words. I could understand the pig language of the *Joshi* (Prison Guards). If you did not do as they commanded, they merely beat you. You learned commands quickly.

I could not quite make out what was going on. Japanese show respect and deference to a person of higher rank by a bow. Lower ranks initiate the bow, like lower ranks in the American Military salute first to higher. In unison, all the Japs were bowing and scraping to a radio. Only one man would they do that for. The Emperor.

I walked back with my cooking water to my fellow POWs at the warehouse and, with them, watched the guards standing silently. Though I strained to hear, I could not understand the message. We stood, awaiting our daily work orders, then sat down to eat our half-cup of weevily rice ration for the day. A guard finally came to us.

"The war is over." His face showed no emotion. Just the fact.

"Oh, yeah?" We could not believe it.

"Yeah. The war is over. You will be home by Thanksgiving."

"Well, how 'bout that?" We did not know what to say, or if even if we should believe him. In his presence we dare not smile or smirk. The question: Who won? We thought it might be a trick to murder us all because we were right at the edge of the mountains, and when the Americans made a landing, we would either be murdered or used as hostages. Later we discovered that a written order had been issued to execute all prisoners before the Allies landed. We were destined to be done away with.

They took us back out to our POW camp, and assigned us no work. As word filtered through the camp we first talked, then were all were hooting and hollering. The war was over! One of the guys walked out of the barracks, and looked at the front gate.

"Our guards are all gone," he said, "the guard shack's empty."

"Hey, the guards are gone. The guards are gone," he hollered. We looked out further to the towers, and no guards were there either.

We jumped up and ran out. Everybody ran around trying to see what was going on. There were no guards anywhere, and this was late afternoon.

The old Chief Petty Officer said, "Well, we'd better set up a guard detail." We had been under guard twenty-four hours a day for more than three years and now felt it was a necessity of life; so we put some men on guard in the guard shack. We did not have any guns, so we "guarded ourselves" with broomstick play rifles.

Twelve
A Little Flag Flapping

Our final "guest of the Emperor" barracks were in a rice paddy surrounded by an eight-foot wooden fence with guard towers and floodlights. A narrow path inside the fence led to the door of showers. Two hundred yards away on one side sat Jap troops with an antiaircraft battery. We knew where they were; they knew where we were.

The celebration of shouts died away only because epidemic hoarseness tempered with smiles had in due time set in. Talk of going home suppressed the agony of hunger and lice. We settled into our barracks and allotted bed slots and almost expected to hear the command for *tenko* that ordinarily came at about this time. It was 8:30 P.M. and dark outside.

All of a sudden we heard this whooping, hollering, and carrying on out front. The guys went running outside, looking around. A Caucasian man stood on the outside of the gate in a uniform, fresh, pressed, and untattered—a complete U.S. Navy officer's uniform. Oak leaf clusters on his collar sparkled in the shine of bright prison lights. His Navy hat identified him as American.

"Hey! He's a free American. He's a free American!" The guys were hollering beyond hoarseness and crowding around.

I do not recall whether he was a commander or a lieutenant commander, but that guy had guts. He had flown off an American carrier and landed in a civilian air strip three miles away. Protected only with a sidearm, he had walked alone to our unmarked camp in the dark of night. Our guards saw him only when he appeared in the glare of our guard-house lights. He was there to check out the barracks, since they had been spotted from the air and were thought to be a POW camp.

The first guy to see him had said, "Holy God! We got the man here at last," and questioned him, "Are you a free American?"

"Yes," he said, "I'm a free American." He told us the name of his carrier and that our forces knew where we were. He had come specifically to assure us that help was on the way.

"Don't try to leave on your own because you might run into a problem. Just stay put and you will receive orders. Tomorrow, I will have some supplies flown in, so be prepared to receive parachute drops." He told us we would be meeting a hospital ship soon. We all spoke at once, thanking him for finding us. We assured him we would wait for further orders.

"Okay." We all laughed. Then we cheered, especially when he said they would be dropping food the next day.

He thanked us for our cooperation and departed. I was amazed that no one said, "Hey, can I go with you?" Not a soul said that. Not a soul. The last I saw of him was the back of his khaki uniform trailing off into the darkness.

To this day, it bumfuzzles me how that guy had enough guts to fly into enemy territory, get out of a plane, walk three miles down in front of a prison camp with lights glaring, and say, "Hey! Are you guys all right?"

Can you imagine what nerves of steel it took, knowing what he knew about the Kamikazes and everything else? I think that guy should be decorated.

The next day they flew over with dive bombers. Of course, everybody was out whooping and hollering and waving. In the meantime we got a hold of some white paint and the guys painted "POW" on the roofs. We wanted to be darn sure they knew where we were and damn sure they spotted us.

We had been bombed before, but this would be "friendly fire" with food and supplies. About 10:30 that morning the dive bombers arrived, roaring in with full flaps down, like they were coming in for a landing. They flew in as slow as they could, but from the ground it is still kind of fast. They zipped across the rice paddy no more than a hundred feet above the camp. The shingles were about to blow off the barracks. All of the POWs were on the outside waving. You could see the guy in the rear cockpit waving to us in return. What a thrill that was! All Navy.

The planes passed over the camp, making a turn for a run over the camp again. The first one that flew over dropped a message streamer down that hit right in our fifty-foot compound. The message pack was opened and read, "Be prepared to take cover. The next will be a firing run. We have supplies for your camp. Be cautious because these are very dangerous. No chutes."

"No chutes? Ohhh-hhhh-hhh."

"No chutes," we echoed, but laughed as we took cover.

They flew in as slow as they could go, almost to the point of falling out of the sky. With full flaps down, their speed looked like a mile per hour over stall.

The Navy stored flour in fifty-pound metal cans that stood as high as a five-gallon jerry can. This was the first thing I saw dropped.

On the top of the eight-foot wooden camp perimeter fence sat one of the prisoners watching our planes drop all the packages affixed with streamers rather than parachutes.

The wind caught one and sent it spinning so fast it looked like a discus on the loose. The guy on the fence froze as it neatly severed the boards between him and the ground.

He peered in disbelief at the neat space punched in the fence and bent down to view the hole picture of a spinning can flying four feet above the pathway, heading to the showers. The whirling can of wheat flour went across the walk, burst through the wall just below a high window, and hit the shower with a boom. So far, so good, but a guy was in there completing his shower. He emerged looking like the Pillsbury Dough Boy in a meltdown.

The next day they dropped us ham. Then they did that barrel roll, wiggled their wings and took off into the wild blue yonder. You may think they would have dropped us K-rations, but these planes were all dive bombers off a carrier. No K-rations in the Navy, so they dropped us stuff they used aboard a ship: flour, coffee, and some fresh-baked bread.

Soon we got the word that B-29s were going to make a drop with parachutes over in the rice paddies. The planes came in as low and slow as they could go and dropped pallets with all kinds of stuff strapped on them. The chutes could not control the descent rate of the overloaded platforms, so some hit the ground violently and came apart, scattering foodstuffs all over the rice paddy. Hungry us salvaged most of the supplies.

All we got to eat in the preceding three and a half years was basically rice, and in some of the camps there was damn little of that. All of a sudden, we were confronted with a variety of real foods. We opened cans of powdered milk and ate it with a spoon. It actually tasted like ice cream!

I had never seen or tasted K-rations before; this Army delicacy delivered by the Air Corps was excellent! There was this new food, Spam. That was creme deluxe, the top of the line. This was like having a Thanksgiving dinner in a can. We had never tasted anything so good.

Our systems were not calibrated to that kind of food. Its richness gave us diarrhea, but everyone in the prison camp had diarrhea anyway. In the next eight hours, the *benjo*, a slit trench with an outhouse sitting atop, became the social center of the camp, in constant use day and night. Though everyone had the "trots" from eating all that rich food, you just kept on overeating. It was a wonder we did not kill our fool selves.

The third day, the Jap camp commander came back, wearing his little cheese knife. He said that he had direct orders to escort us from the camp to the port where we were to meet the hospital ship. These direct orders came from the Allied Command, and left no allowance for interpretation or deviation. It was the Japanese prison commander's responsibility to guarantee our safety from the civilian population or some zealot not personally recognizing the surrender. He would have Japanese guards accompany us to make sure we were not harmed in any manner.

We knew, because the Emperor of Japan had spoken, that something big had happened. We still did not yet know what it was that made our Jap guards suddenly display a new cultural attitude toward their former POWs.

A Jap guard who spoke some English told us that the Americans had destroyed an entire city with a single bomb from a single plane. He didn't know much more than that. One plane with one bomb taking out one city did not sound plausible to us.

Before we left the prison camp, our tattered rags, home to our many body lice, were exchanged for Japanese Army uniforms with new brown Japanese Army boots. They tended to fit surprisingly well, for two reasons. One, we had lost a lot of weight. Two, these uniforms were apparently reserved for the taller soldiers from the northern part of Japan where some men grew to be six feet tall.

Since we were now in the best of dress, it was time to start our journey to meet our new life as free men. We, under the protection of the now friendly Japanese guards, were loaded on this passenger train and set off for the coast to meet with a U.S. Navy hospital ship. The trip was uneventful, and we arrived at the prearranged location to meet with the medical personnel.

A Chief Boatswain Mate from the hospital ship met us. His assignment was to oversee the handling of the returned POWs. He asked us to fall into columns of fours, and we complied. He called us to attention and welcomed us back to the control of our respective countries.

"Awwright, men," yelled the chief, "we need a head count, so count off."

All the prisoners standing in line were not American. There were about ten different nationalities represented, including British, Australians, Chinese, Korean, Indian, and Javanese. Some had been captured by German raiders on ships at sea and turned over to the Japanese. We had done the same slave labor in the prison camps. So there we were, as we were, staring at the old chief who had us all lined up.

"I need to get a count," he repeats louder. "Count off here."

"One , two . . . *bevvvp, bevvvpp bevvvppp*." Nobody could get it right. We were having a helluva a time trying to count off with all those different nationalities. This was even more frustrating the second and third times around. We were so near yet so far, because they could not get a correct number at muster.

"Hey, chief," called out our old POW chief from the camp, "you want me to get you an accurate count?"

"Please do, if you can," the free chief replied.

Our chief stepped out in front of the group and barked, "*Kou-ski!*" That was the Japanese order for "Attention." Out of habit, the POWs snapped to attention.

"*Bongo!*" he hollered.

"*Ichinee.*"

"*Ni.*"

"*San.*"

We went right on down the line without one bobble or loss of pace to the end. That was so funny. We were not able to count off in English, so we did it in Japanese, like we had for the past few years.

"Well, chief, we got six hundred forty men here."

The free chief wrote it down on his pad, and said, "Alright, men, we'll load out here. Come on." He did not try to march us to the dock with commands in English.

Looking like a bunch of Jap soldiers, we were all lined up on the pier. We stood there in the cool breeze of the bay waiting for the motor launches to arrive and take us out to the hospital ship lying at anchor in the bay. You could see the big red cross showing on her midships.

The motor launches arrived alongside the dock area to pick up the waiting line of men clothed in fresh enemy uniforms. The defeated enemy might have had further "loss of face" if the ragged, ratty nature of our lice-infested prison garb had been on display to the world.

There, at the stern of the launch, freely flapping in the Japanese breeze was an American flag, the first one we had observed in over three years.

A little flag fluttering in the breeze can be such a small event. Most people at home might not pay it much attention. But for someone pledged to protect our nation who had not seen the flag fly in several years, that little banner gave us all a rush of feelings. Especially when, during our imprisonment, to have flown or appreciated its flying would have invited torture and death.

Each star of the forty-eight in the field of blue supported by crisp lines of red and white became a blur, for silently and in a moment of personal national reverence on that foreign soil, we were given the instant understanding of the freedom our flag stood for. The moment was etched into each of our minds personally. I will always remember that event, much like the majority of my generation will remember what they were doing on December 7, 1941.

Any moment of beauty must pass: The "I do" of a wedding gives way to the workings of a marriage. The cry of a newborn leads to the rearing of a child. The idle of a naval launch accepting misty-eyed passengers led to the roar of engines transporting us to the hospital ship.

"We are free! We are free! God bless America."

Epilogue

As part of a nation unprepared for war in 1941, those of us who were captured early on Bataan and Corregidor felt twice forgotten—once as "help is on the way" went not to us but to not-so-nearby Australia and twice as we were imprisoned on the mainland of Japan, and fell within the Allied bombing patterns during the course of the war. We felt remembered with our release from the brutality of slavery and beatings; and with the "bombing runs" of food to our POW camps; and reinstated upon glimpsing a small U.S. flag fluttering in the Japanese breeze as we left that island.

Later, as a nation prepared for war, America would fly twenty-four-hour-a-day armed missions with atomic weaponry for instant use for some forty-four years running, ceasing only after the Berlin Wall came down, when such preparedness was deemed unnecessary. As nations now largely composed of people born after World War II, the personal effect on this history is being replaced by that learned from books, TV, movies, or the internet. With the gentle, polite Japanese of today, it is difficult to believe the actions of the harsh, brutal, vicious Japs of that period existed. They did, and this is one of millions of stories out there testifying to that era of human relationships. Its purpose is to identify actions that happened, not to condemn generations of people yet to be born afterward. It is to remind us that in coming to today's live-in-the-present attitude underlying "trading partner" relationships, there was a horrible disruption of humanity mollified by history often re-written as merely a "glitch in relationships."

The suddenness of World War II's start, seen by America on December 7, 1941, was matched by the suddenness of its end, seen by Japan on August 15, 1945. My life was one of more than 100,000 POWs instantly saved by the bombing of Hiroshima, negating their order to murder us first upon the invasion of the island. Estimates of that time say 500,000 invading Allied lives were saved, and four million Japs were salvaged to become four million Japanese inhabitants on the island of Japan whose culture evolved to that which we know today. I shall be forever thankful for the group who delivered "the gadget" to Hiroshima, and Nagasaki; their collective "working name" by inventors before becoming the atomic bomb.

The purpose in telling my experience is to remind us of that era past so that some history might not be once forgotten, much less—twice forgotten.

Erwin C. Winkel II, M.D.
Co-author